MAC OS® X LION

Simplified®

Visual

by Paul McFedries

WILEY

John Wiley & Sons, Inc.

MAC OS® X LION SIMPLIFIED®

Published by
John Wiley & Sons, Inc.
10475 Crosspoint Boulevard
Indianapolis, IN 46256

www.wiley.com

Published simultaneously in Canada

Wiley also publishes its books in a variety of electronic formats and by print-on-demand. Some content that appears in standard print versions of this book may not be available in other formats. For more information about Wiley products, visit us at www.wiley.com.

Library of Congress Control Number: 2011934631

ISBN: 978-1-118-02240-5

Manufactured in the United States of America

10 9 8 7 6 5 4 3 2 1

Trademark Acknowledgments

Contact Us

For general information on our other products and services please contact our Customer Care Department within the U.S. at 877-762-2974, outside the U.S. at 317-572-3993 or fax 317-572-4002.

For technical support please visit www.wiley.com/techsupport.

WILEY

John Wiley & Sons, Inc.

Sales
Contact Wiley
at (877) 762-2974 or
fax (317) 572-4002.

Credits

Executive Editor
Jody Lefevere

Project Editor
Lynn Northrup

Technical Editor
Dennis R. Cohen

Editorial Director
Robyn Siesky

Business Manager
Amy Knies

Senior Marketing Manager
Sandy Smith

Vice President and Executive Group Publisher
Richard Swadley

Vice President and Executive Publisher
Barry Pruett

Senior Project Coordinator
Kristie Rees

Graphics and Production Specialist
Andrea Hornberger

Quality Control Technician
Lindsay Amones

Proofreading and Indexing
Melissa D. Buddendeck
BIM Indexing & Proofreading Services

Screen Artists
Ana Carillo
Cheryl Grubbs

Special Help
Rebekah Worthman

About the Author

Paul McFedries is a technical writer who has been authoring computer books since 1991. He has more than 70 books to his credit, which together have sold more than four million copies worldwide. These books include the Wiley titles *Teach Yourself VISUALLY Macs, Second Edition; MacBook Air Portable Genius, Second Edition; iPhone 4 Portable Genius;* and *Macs Portable Genius, Second Edition.* Paul also runs Word Spy, a website dedicated to tracking new words and phrases (see www.wordspy.com). Please visit Paul's personal website at www.mcfedries.com, or follow him on twitter at www.twitter.com/paulmcf and www.twitter.com/wordspy.

Author's Acknowledgments

The book you hold in your hands is not only an excellent learning tool, but it is truly beautiful, as well. I am happy to have supplied the text that you will read, but the beautiful layout and colors come from Wiley's crack team of graphics specialists. The scope of the tasks, the accuracy of the spelling and grammar, and the veracity of the information are all the result of hard work performed by project editor Lynn Northrup and technical editor Dennis Cohen. Thanks to both of you for your excellent work. My thanks, as well, to acquisitions editor Jody Lefevere for asking me to write this book.

How to Use This Book

Who This Book Is For

This book is for the reader who has never used this particular technology or software application. It is also for readers who want to expand their knowledge.

The Conventions in This Book

❶ Steps

This book uses a step-by-step format to guide you easily through each task. Numbered steps are actions you must do; bulleted steps clarify a point, step, or optional feature; and indented steps give you the result.

❷ Notes

Notes give additional information — special conditions that may occur during an operation, a situation that you want to avoid, or a cross reference to a related area of the book.

❸ Icons and Buttons

Icons and buttons show you exactly what you need to click to perform a step.

❹ Simplify It

Simplify It sections offer additional information, including warnings and shortcuts.

❺ Bold

Bold type shows command names, options, and text or numbers you must type.

❻ Italics

Italic type introduces and defines a new term.

Table of Contents

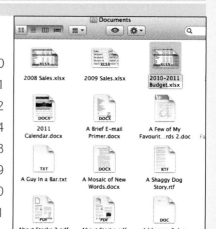

3

Surfing the World Wide Web

4

Communicating via E-mail

Table of Contents

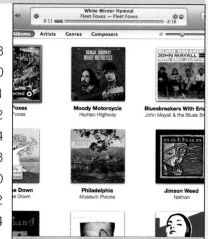

7

Synchronizing an iPod, iPhone, or iPad

8

Viewing and Editing Photos

Table of Contents

9

Playing and Creating Digital Video

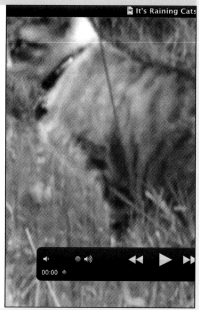

10

Customizing Mac OS X to Suit Your Style

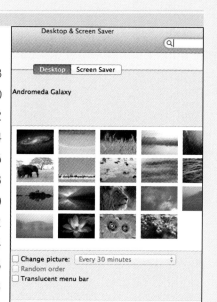

11

Performing Mac OS X Maintenance

12

Troubleshooting Mac OS X Problems

Chapter 1

Learning Basic Mac OS X Program Tasks

The Mac OS X operating system is installed on all new Macintosh computers. If you already have an Intel-based Mac, you can purchase the latest version — Mac OS X Lion — and install it.

One of the most crucial Mac OS X concepts is the application (also sometimes called a program) because it is via applications that you perform all other Mac OS X tasks. Therefore, it is important to have a basic understanding of how to start and manage applications in Mac OS X.

Explore the Mac OS X Screen

Before you can begin to understand how the Mac OS X operating system works, you should become familiar with the basic screen elements.

These elements include the Mac OS X menu bar, the desktop, desktop icons, and the Dock.

Understanding where these elements appear on the screen and what they are used for will help you work through the rest of the tasks in this book and will help you navigate Mac OS X and its applications on your own.

Menu Bar

The menu bar contains the pull-down menus for Mac OS X and most Mac software.

Desktop

This is the Mac OS X work area, where you work with your applications and documents.

Mouse Pointer

When you move your mouse, the pointer moves along with it.

Desktop Icon

An icon on the desktop represents an application, a folder, a document, or a device attached to your Mac, such as a disk drive, a CD or DVD, or an iPod.

Dock

The Dock contains several icons, each of which gives you quick access to some commonly used applications.

Tour the Dock

The Dock is the strip that runs along the bottom of the Mac screen. The Dock is populated with several small images, each of which is called an *icon*. Each icon represents a particular component of your Mac — an application, a folder, a document, and so on — and clicking the icon opens the component.

This makes the Dock one of the most important and useful Mac OS X features because it gives you one-click access to applications, folders, and documents.

The icons shown here are typical, but your Mac may display a different arrangement.

Finder
Work with the files on your computer.

Launchpad
View, organize, and start your applications.

Mission Control
Organize your open windows.

App Store
Install new applications and upgrade existing applications.

Dashboard
Access several cool and handy mini applications called *widgets*.

Mail
Send and receive e-mail messages.

Safari
Browse the World Wide Web on the Internet.

iChat
Converse with other people in real time by sending each other text messages.

FaceTime
Place video calls to other FaceTime users.

Address Book
Store people's names, addresses, and other contact information.

iCal
Record upcoming appointments, birthdays, meetings, and other events.

Preview
View certain files on your Mac, particularly photos.

iTunes
Play music and other media and add media to your iPod, iPhone, or iPad.

Photo Booth
Take a picture using your Mac's camera.

iPhoto
Import and edit digital photos and other images.

iMovie
Import video footage and edit your own digital movies.

GarageBand
Create songs, podcasts, and other audio files.

Time Machine
Create and access backups of your files.

System Preferences
Customize and configure your Mac.

Applications
Display the contents of your Applications folder.

Documents
Display the contents of your Documents folder.

Downloads
Display the contents of your Downloads folder.

Trash
Delete files, folders, and applications.

Start an Application

To perform tasks of any kind in Mac OS X, you use one of the applications installed on your Mac. The application you use depends on the task you want to perform. For example, if you want to surf the World Wide Web, you would use a web browser application, such as the Safari program that comes with Mac OS X.

Before you can use an application, however, you must first tell Mac OS X which application you want to run. Mac OS X launches the application and displays it on the desktop. You can then use the application's tools to perform your tasks.

Start an Application

1 Click the **Finder** icon (🌐).

Note: *If the application that you want to start has an icon in the Dock, you can click the icon to start the application and skip the rest of these steps.*

The Finder window appears.

2 Click **Applications**.

Note: *You can also navigate to Applications in any Finder window by pressing* Shift *+* ⌘ *+* A *or by clicking* **Go** *and then clicking* **Applications** *from Finder's menu bar.*

The Applications window appears.

③ Double-click the icon of the application that you want to start.

Note: If you see a folder icon ( ), it means that the application resides in its own folder, a storage area on the computer. Double-click to open the folder and then double-click the application icon.

● The application appears on the desktop.

● Mac OS X adds a button for the application to the Dock.

● The menu bar displays the menus associated with the application.

Simplify It

How do I add an icon to the Dock for an application I use frequently?
First, start the application as described in Steps **1** to **3**. Right-click the application's Dock icon, click **Options**, and then click **Keep in Dock**.

How do I shut down a running application?
The easiest way is to right-click the application's Dock icon and then click **Quit**. Alternatively, you can switch to the application and press + .

Start an Application Using Launchpad

You can also start an application using the Launchpad feature that is new for Mac OS X Lion. This is often faster than using the Applications folder as described in the previous section, particularly for applications that do not have a Dock icon.

Launchpad is designed to mimic the Home screens of the iPhone, iPad, and iPhone touch. So if you own one or more of these devices, then you are already familiar with how Launchpad works.

Start an Application Using Launchpad

1 Click the **Launchpad** icon (⬜).

The Launchpad screen appears.

2 If the application you want to start resides in a different Launchpad screen, click the dot that corresponds to the screen.

Launchpad switches to the screen and displays the applications.

③ If the application you want to start resides within a folder, click the folder.

Launchpad opens the folder.

④ Click the icon of the application you want to start.

Mac OS X starts the application.

The dots that represent each Launchpad screen are quite small, making them hard to click with the mouse. Is there an easier way to navigate the Launchpad screens?
Yes. I mentioned earlier that Mac OS X Lion has designed Launchpad to look somewhat similar to the Home screens of the iPhone, iPad, and iPhone touch. Another similarity is how you navigate the screens.

On an iPhone, iPad, and iPhone touch, you navigate the Home screens by using a finger to swipe the screen right or left. With your Mac, you can also navigate the Launchpad screens by swiping. In this case, however, you must use two fingers, and you swipe right or left on either the trackpad or the surface of a Magic Mouse.

Switch Between Applications

If you plan on running multiple applications at the same time, you need to know how to easily switch from one application to another.

In Mac OS X, after you start one application, you do not need to close that application before you open another one. Mac OS X supports a feature called *multitasking*, which means running two or more applications at once. This is handy if you need to use several applications throughout the day. For example, you might keep your word processing application, your web browser, and your e-mail application open all day.

Switch Between Applications

1 Click the Dock icon of the application that you want to switch to.

● Mac OS X brings the application's window(s) to the foreground.

● The menu bar displays the menus associated with the application.

Note: To switch between applications from the keyboard, press and hold ⌘ and repeatedly press Tab *until the application that you want is highlighted in the list of running applications. Release* ⌘ *to switch to the application.*

View Running Applications with Mission Control

The Mission Control feature, which is new in Mac OS X Lion, makes it easier for you to navigate and locate your running applications.

Mac OS X allows you to open multiple applications at once, and the only real limit to the number of open applications you can have is the amount of memory contained in your

Mac. In practical terms, this means you can easily open a half a dozen or more applications, some of which may have multiple open windows. To help locate and navigate to the window you need, use the Mission Control feature.

View Running Applications with Mission Control

① Click **Mission Control** in the Dock.

Note: You can also invoke Mission Control by pressing F9 or, depending on how your keyboard is configured, Fn + F9.

● Mission Control displays each open window.

● Mission Control groups windows from the same application.

To switch to a particular window, click it.

● To close Mission Control without selecting a window, click **Desktop** or press Esc.

Tour an Application Window

When you start an application, it appears on the Mac OS X desktop in its own window. Each application has a unique window layout, but almost all application windows have a few features in common.

To get the most out of your applications and to start working quickly and efficiently in an application, you need to know what these common features are and where to find them within the application window.

Close Button

Click the **Close** button ( ) to remove the application window from the desktop, usually without exiting the application.

Minimize Button

Click the **Minimize** button ( ) to remove the window from the desktop and display an icon for the currently open document in the right side of the Dock. The window is still open, but not active.

Zoom Button

Click the **Zoom** button ( ) to enlarge the window so that it can display all of its content, or as much of its content as can fit the screen.

Toolbar

The toolbar contains buttons that offer easy access to common application commands and features, although not all applications have toolbars. To move the window, click and drag the toolbar.

Status Bar

The status bar displays information about the current state of the application or document.

Vertical Scrollbar

Use the vertical scrollbar to navigate up and down in a document. Click **Scroll Up** ( ) to navigate up; click **Scroll Down** ( ) to navigate down.

Horizontal Scrollbar

Use the horizontal scrollbar to navigate left and right in a document. Click **Scroll Left** ( ) to navigate left, and click **Scroll Right** ( ) to navigate right.

Resize Control

Click and drag   in the lower right corner of the window to make the window larger or smaller.

Run an Application Full Screen

You can maximize the viewing and working areas of an application by running that application in full-screen mode. When you switch to full-screen mode, Mac OS X hides the menu bar, the application's status bar, the Dock, and the top section of the application window (the section that includes the Close,

Minimize, and Zoom icons). Mac OS X then expands the rest of the application window so that it takes up the entire screen.

You must be running Mac OS X Lion to use full-screen mode. Note, too, that not all programs are capable of switching to full-screen mode.

Run an Application Full Screen

1 Click **View**.

2 Click **Enter Full Screen**.

● You can also hold down Option and click 🔲.

Mac OS X expands the application window to take up the entire screen.

Note: To exit full-screen mode, move the mouse ⟍ up to the top of the screen to reveal the menu bar, click **View**, and then click **Exit Full Screen**.

Select a Command from a Pull-Down Menu

When you are working in an application, you can use the menu bar to access the application's commands and features.

Each item in the menu bar represents a *pull-down menu*, a collection of commands usually related to each other in some way.

For example, the File menu commands usually deal with file-related tasks such as opening and closing documents.

The items in a menu are either commands that execute an action in the application, or features that you can turn on and off.

Select a Command from a Pull-Down Menu

Execute Commands

1 Click the name of the menu that you want to display.

● The application displays the menu.

2 Click the command that you want to execute.

The application executes the command.

● If a command is followed by an ellipsis (...), it means the command displays a dialog.

● If a command is followed by an arrow (▸), it means the command displays a submenu. Click the command to open the submenu and then click the command that you want to run.

Turn Features On and Off

1 Click the name of the menu that you want to display.

● The application displays the menu.

2 Click the menu item.

You may have to click for a submenu if your command is not on the main menu.

The application turns the feature either on (a check mark (✓) appears the next time you open the menu) or off (no check mark appears the next time you open the menu).

Select a Command Using a Toolbar

You can access many application commands faster by using the toolbar. Many applications come with a toolbar, which is a collection of buttons, lists, and other controls displayed in a strip, usually across the top of the application window.

Because the toolbar is always visible, you can always use it to select commands, which means that the toolbar often gives you one-click access to the application's most common features. This is faster than using the menu bar method, which often takes several clicks, depending on the command.

Select a Command Using a Toolbar

Turn Features On and Off

1 Click the toolbar button that represents the feature you want to turn on.

● The application turns the feature on and indicates this state by highlighting the toolbar button.

● When a feature is turned off, the application does not highlight the button.

Execute Commands

1 Click the toolbar button that represents the command that you want.

2 If the button displays a menu, click the command on the menu.

● The application executes the command.

Select Options with Dialog Controls

You often interact with an application by selecting options or typing text using a dialog.

A *dialog* is a small window that appears when an application has information for you, or needs you to provide information. For example, when you select the File menu's Print command to print a document, you use the Print dialog to specify the number of copies that you want to print.

You provide that and other information by accessing various types of dialog controls. To provide information to an application quickly and accurately, you need to know what these dialog controls look like and how they work.

Command Button

Clicking a command button executes the command written on the button face. For example, you can click **OK** to apply settings that you have chosen in a dialog, or you can click **Cancel** to close the dialog without changing the settings.

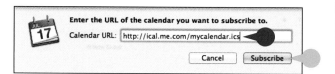

Text Box

A text box enables you to enter typed text. Use the `Del` key to delete any existing characters, and then type your text.

List Box

A list box displays a list of choices from which you select the item you want. Use the vertical scrollbar to bring the item you want into view, and then click the item to select it.

Tabs

Many dialogs offer a large number of controls, so related controls appear on different tabs, and the tab names and icons appear across the top of the dialog. Click a tab to see its controls.

Pop-Up Menu

A pop-up menu displays a list of choices from which you select the item you want. Click ⫶ to pop up the menu, and then click the item that you want to select.

Check Box

Clicking a check box toggles an application feature on and off. If you are turning on a feature, the check box changes from ☐ to ☑; if you are turning off the feature, the check box changes from ☑ to ☐.

Radio Button

Clicking a radio button turns on an application feature. Only one radio button in a group can be turned on at a time. When you click a radio button that is currently off, it changes from ○ to ⊙; a radio button that is on changes from ⊙ to ○.

Chapter 2

Learning Basic Mac OS X Document Tasks

Much of the work you do in Mac OS X will involve documents, which are files that contain text, images, and other data. These tasks include saving your work, opening a document to view or make changes to it, printing a document, and editing a document.

Your documents are stored on your Mac as files, and Mac OS X also offers tools for working with these files. These tools enable you to copy or move a file, rename a file, or delete a file. To perform these and other tasks, it is important to have a basic understanding of how to work with and manage documents in Mac OS X.

Save a Document

After you create a document and make changes to it, you can save the document to preserve your work.

When you work on a document, Mac OS X stores the changes in your computer's memory. However, Mac OS X erases the contents of the Mac's memory each time you shut down or restart the computer. This means that the changes you have made to your document are lost when you turn off or restart your Mac.

However, saving the document preserves your changes on your Mac's hard disk.

Save a Document

① Click **File**.

② Click **Save**.

In most applications, you can also press ⌘ + Ⓢ.

If you have saved the document previously, your changes are now preserved, and you do not need to follow the rest of the steps in this section.

If this is a new document that you have never saved before, the Save dialog appears.

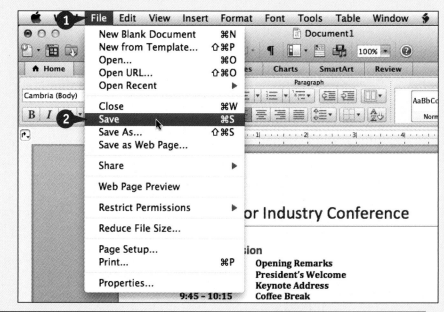

③ Use the Save As text box to type the filename you want to use.

● To store the file in a different folder, you can click ⇕ in the Where list and then click the location that you prefer.

④ Click **Save**.

The application saves the file.

Open a Document

To work with a document that you have saved in the past, you can open it in the application that you used to create it.

When you save a document, you save its contents to your Mac's hard disk, and those contents are stored in a separate file. When you open the document using the same application that you used to save it, Mac OS X loads the file's contents into memory and displays the document in the application. You can then view or edit the document as needed.

Open a Document

① Start the application that you want to work with.

② Click **File**.

③ Click **Open**.

In most applications, you can also press ⌘ + O.

The Open dialog appears.

● To select a different folder from which to open the file, you can click ⁞ and then click the location that you prefer.

④ Click the document.

⑤ Click **Open**.

The document appears in the application window.

Print a Document

When you need a hard copy of your document, either for your files or to distribute to someone else, you can send the document to your printer.

Most applications that deal with documents also come with a Print command. When you run this command, the Print dialog appears. You use the Print dialog to choose the printer you want to use as well as to specify how many copies you want to print. Many Print dialogs also enable you to see a preview of your document before printing it.

Print a Document

1 Turn on your printer.

2 Open the document that you want to print.

3 Click **File**.

4 Click **Print**.

In many applications, you can select the Print command by pressing ⌘ + P.

The Print dialog appears.

The layout of the Print dialog varies from application to application. The version shown here is a typical example.

5 If you have more than one printer, click ‡ in the Printer list to select the printer that you want to use.

● To print more than one copy, click **Show Details** (in some cases, you click ⬇ to expand the dialog instead) and then use the Copies text box to type the number of copies to print.

6 Click **Print**.

● Mac OS X prints the document. The printer's icon appears in the Dock while the document prints.

Simplify It

Can I preview my document before I print it?
Yes. It is a good idea to preview the document before printing it to ensure that the document layout looks the way you want. To preview the document, follow Steps **1** to **4** in this section to display the Print dialog. Click **Preview** to display the document in the Preview application. When you are done, click **Preview** and then click **Quit Preview**.

Edit Document Text

When you work with a character-based file, such as a text or word processing document or an e-mail message, you need to know the basic techniques for editing, selecting, copying, and moving text.

It is rare that any text you enter into a document is perfect the first time through. It is far more likely that the text contains errors that require correcting, or words, sentences, or paragraphs that appear in the wrong place.

To get your document text the way you want it, you need to know how to edit text, including deleting characters, selecting the text you want to work with, and copying and moving text.

Delete Characters

1 In a text document, click immediately to the right of the last character that you want to delete.

● The cursor appears after the character.

Agenda for Industry Conference

Morning Session

8:00 – 8:30	Opening Remarks
8:30 – 9:00	President's Welcome
9:00 – 9:45	Keynote Address
9:45 – 10:15	Coffee Break
10:15 – 11:00	Industry Trends
11:00 – 12:00	Advisory Panel
12:00 – 1:30	Lunch

Afternoon Session

1:30 – 3:00	Breakout Sessions
3:00 – 3:30	Coffee Break
3:30 – 4:30	A Look at the Future of the Industry **1**

2 Press Del until you have deleted all the characters you want.

If you make a mistake, immediately click **Edit**, and then click **Undo**. You can also press ⌘ + Z.

Agenda for Industry Conference

Morning Session

8:00 – 8:30	Opening Remarks
8:30 – 9:00	President's Welcome
9:00 – 9:45	Keynote Address
9:45 – 10:15	Coffee Break
10:15 – 11:00	Industry Trends
11:00 – 12:00	Advisory Panel
12:00 – 1:30	Lunch

Afternoon Session

1:30 – 3:00	Breakout Sessions
3:00 – 3:30	Coffee Break
3:30 – 4:30	A Look at the Future **2**

Agenda for Industry Conference

Morning Session

8:00 – 8:30	**Opening Remarks**
8:30 – 9:00	**President's Welcome**
9:00 – 9:45	**Keynote Address**
9:45 – 10:15	**Coffee Break**
10:15 – 11:00	**Industry Trends**
11:00 – 12:00	**Advisory Panel**
12:00 – 1:30	**Lunch**

Afternoon Session

1:30 – 3:00	**Breakout Sessions**
3:00 – 3:30	**Coffee Break**
3:30 – 4:30	**A Look at the Future**

 Agenda for Industry Conference

Morning Session

8:00 – 8:30	**Opening Remarks**
8:30 – 9:00	**President's Welcome**
9:00 – 9:45	**Keynote Address**
9:45 – 10:15	**Coffee Break**
10:15 – 11:00	**Industry Trends**
11:00 – 12:00	**Advisory Panel**
12:00 – 1:30	**Lunch**

Afternoon Session

1:30 – 3:00	**Breakout Sessions**
3:00 – 3:30	**Coffee Break**
3:30 – 4:30	**A Look at the Future**

Select Text for Editing

1 Click and drag across the text that you want to select.

2 Release the mouse button.

● The application highlights the selected text.

Simplify It

Are there any shortcut methods for selecting text?
Yes, most Mac OS X applications have shortcuts you can use. Here are the most useful ones:

● Double-click a word to select it.
● Hold down **Shift** and press ➡ or ⬅ to select entire words.
● Hold down **Shift** and **⌘** and press ➡ to select to the end of the line, or ⬅ to select to the beginning of the line.
● Triple-click inside a paragraph to select it.
● Click **Edit** and then click **Select All**, or press **⌘** + **A** to select the entire document.

continued

Edit Document Text *(continued)*

Once you select text, you can then copy or move the text to another location in your document.

Copying text is often a useful way to save work. For example, if you want to use the same passage of text elsewhere in the document, you can copy it instead of typing

it from scratch. Similarly, if you need a similar passage in another part of the document, copy the original and then edit the copy as needed.

If you entered a passage of text in the wrong position within the document, you can fix that by moving the text to the correct location.

Copy Text

① Select the text that you want to copy.

② Click **Edit**.

③ Click **Copy**.

In most applications, you can also press ⌘ + ©.

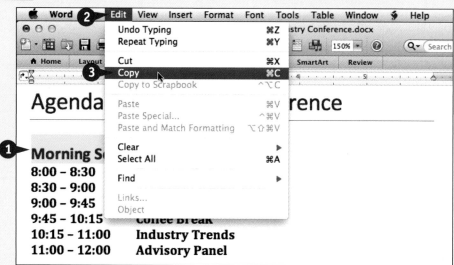

④ Click inside the document where you want the copied text to appear.

The cursor appears in the position where you clicked.

⑤ Click **Edit**.

⑥ Click **Paste**.

In most applications, you can also press ⌘ + ⓥ.

● The application inserts a copy of the selected text at the cursor position.

Move Text

1 Select the text that you want to move.

2 Click **Edit**.

3 Click **Cut**.

In most applications, you can also press ⌘ + X.

The application removes the text from the document.

4 Click inside the document where you want to move the text.

The cursor appears at the position where you clicked.

5 Click **Edit**.

6 Click **Paste**.

In most applications, you can also press ⌘ + .

● The application inserts the text at the cursor position.

Simplify It

How do I move and copy text with my mouse?
First, select the text that you want to move or copy. To move the selected text, position the mouse pointer over the selection and then click and drag the text to the new position within the document.

To copy the selected text, position the mouse pointer over the selection, press and hold the Option key, and then click and drag the text (the mouse ▸ changes to ▹) to the new position within the document.

Afternoon Session		
12:00 – 1:30	Lunch	
1:30 – 3:00	Breakout Sessions	
3:00 – 3:30	Coffee Break	
3:30 – 4:30	A Look at the Future	

Day Two

Morning Session

Afternoon Session		
8:00 – 1:30	Lunch	
1:30 – 3:00	Breakout Sessions	
3:00 – 3:30	Coffee Break	
3:30 – 4:30	A Look at the Future	

Copy a File

You can use Mac OS X to make an exact copy of a file. This is useful when you want to make an extra copy of an important file to use as a backup. Similarly, you might require a copy of a file if you want to send the copy on a disk to another person. Finally, copying a file is also a real timesaver if you need a new file very similar to an existing file: You copy the original file and then make the required changes to the copy.

You can copy either a single file or multiple files. You can also use this technique to copy a folder.

Copy a File

1 Locate the file that you want to copy.

2 Open the folder to which you want to copy the file.

To open a second folder window, click **File** and then click **New Finder Window**, or press ⌘ + N.

3 Press and hold the Option key, and then click and drag the file and drop it inside the destination folder.

● The original file remains in its folder.

● A copy of the original file appears in the destination folder.

You can also make a copy of a file in the same folder, which is useful if you want to make major changes to the file and you would like to preserve a copy of the original. Click the file, click **File**, and then click **Duplicate**, or press ⌘ + D. Mac OS X creates a copy with the word "copy" added to the filename.

Move a File

When you need to store a file in a new location, the easiest way is to move the file from its current folder to another folder on your Mac.

When you save a file for the first time, you specify a folder on your Mac's hard disk. This original location is not permanent, however. Using the technique in this section, you can move the file to another location on your Mac's hard disk.

You can use this technique to move a single file, multiple files, and even a folder.

Move a File

① Locate the file that you want to move.

② Open the folder to which you want to move the file.

To create a new destination folder in the current folder, click **File** and then click **New Folder**, or press Shift + ⌘ + N.

③ Click and drag the file and drop it inside the destination folder.

Note: *If you are moving the file to another disk drive, you must hold down ⌘ while you click and drag the file.*

● The file disappears from its original folder.

● The file moves to the destination folder.

Rename a File

You can change the name of a file, which is useful if the current filename does not accurately describe the contents of the file. By giving your document a descriptive name, you make it easier to find the file later.

You should rename only those documents that you have created or that have been given to you by someone else. Do not try to rename any of the Mac OS X system files or any files associated with your applications, or your computer may behave erratically, or even crash.

Rename a File

1 Open the folder containing the file that you want to rename.

2 Click the file.

3 Press Return.

● A text box appears around the filename.

You can also rename any folders that you have created.

4 Edit the existing name or type a new name that you want to use for the file.

If you decide that you do not want to rename the file after all, you can press Esc to cancel the operation.

5 Press Return or click an empty section of the folder.

● The new name appears under the file icon.

Delete
a File

When you no longer need a file, you can delete it. This helps to prevent your hard drive from becoming cluttered with unnecessary files.

You should ensure that you delete only those documents that you have created or that have

been given to you by someone else. Do not delete any of the Mac OS X system files or any files associated with your applications, or your computer may behave erratically, or even crash.

Delete a File

1 Locate the file that you want to delete.

2 Click and drag the file and drop it on the Trash icon in the Dock.

● The file disappears from the folder.

You can also delete a file by clicking it and then pressing ⌘ + Del.

If you delete a file accidentally, you can restore it. Simply click the Dock's Trash icon to open the Trash window. Click and drag the file from the Trash window and drop it back in its original folder.

Chapter 3

Surfing the World Wide Web

The *World Wide Web*, or simply, the web, is a massive storehouse of information that resides on computers, called web servers, located all over the world. Information is presented on web pages that you download to your computer using a web browser program, such the Mac OS X Safari application. Each web page can combine text with images, sounds, music, and even videos to present information on a particular subject. A *website* is a collection of web pages associated with a particular person or organization.

If your Mac is connected to the Internet, you can use the Safari browser to navigate — or *surf* — websites.

Open and Close Safari

To access websites and view web pages, you must use a web browser program. In Mac OS X, the default web browser is Safari, which you can use to surf websites when your Mac is connected to the Internet.

The Safari application offers a number of features that make it easier to browse the web. For example, you can open multiple pages in a single Safari window, you can save your favorite sites for easier access, and you can perform Internet searches from the Safari window.

To use these features, you must know how to start the Safari application. When you have finished surfing the web, you also need to know how to shut down Safari to save system resources on your Mac.

Open and Close Safari

Open Safari

1 In the Dock, click the **Safari** icon (⬤).

The Safari window appears.

Note: The initial web page you see depends on how your version of Safari has been configured. In most cases, you see the Apple.com Start page.

Close Safari

1 Click **Safari**.

2 Click **Quit Safari**.

Are there other methods I can use to open Safari?
If you have removed the 🧭 icon from the Dock, there are a couple of other methods you can use to start Safari. If you have used Safari recently, click 🍎, click **Recent Items**, and then click **Safari**. You can also click **Spotlight** (🔍), type **Safari**, and then click **Safari** in the search results.

Are there faster methods I can use to close Safari?
Probably the fastest method you can use to quit Safari is to right-click its icon (🧭) and then click **Quit**. If your hands are closer to the keyboard than to the mouse, you can quit Safari by switching to the application and then pressing ⌘ + Q.

Select a Link

Almost all web pages include links to other pages that contain related information. When you select a link, your web browser loads the other page.

Web page links come in two forms: text and images. Text links consist of a word or phrase that usually appears underlined and in a different color from the rest of the page text.

However, web page designers can control the look of their links, so text links may not always stand out in this way.

Therefore, knowing which words, phrases, or images are links is not always obvious. The only way to tell for sure is to position the mouse (↖) over the text or image; if the ↖ changes to 👆, you know the item is a link.

Select a Link

1 Position ↖ over the link
(↖ changes to 👆).

2 Click the text or image.

⬤ The status bar shows the address of the linked page.

> **Note:** *The address shown in the status bar when you point at a link may be different from the one shown when the page is downloading. This occurs when the website "redirects" the link.*

> **Note:** *If you do not see the status bar, click* **View** *then click* **Show Status Bar***.*

The linked web page appears.

⬤ The status bar shows the current download status.

⬤ The web page title and address change after the linked page is loaded.

Enter a Web Page Address

If you know the address of a specific web page, you can type it into the web browser to display the page. Every web page is uniquely identified by an address called the Uniform Resource Locator, or URL (pronounced *yoo-ar-ell* or *erl*).

The URL is composed of four basic parts: the *transfer method* (usually HTTP, which stands for Hypertext Transfer Protocol), the website

domain name, the *directory* where the web page is located on the server, and the *web page filename*.

The website domain name suffix most often used is .com (commercial), but other common suffixes include .gov (government), .org (nonprofit organization), .edu (education), and country domains such as .ca (Canada).

Enter a Web Page Address

1. Click inside the address bar.

2. Press **Del** to delete the existing address.

3. Type the address of the web page you want to visit.

4. Press **Return**.

The web page appears.

● The web page title changes after the page is loaded.

Open a Web Page in a Tab

You can make it easier to work with multiple web pages and sites simultaneously by opening each page in its own tab. As you surf the web, you may come upon a page that you want to keep available while you visit other sites. That page may contain important information that you need to reference, or it might be a page that you want to read later on.

Instead of leaving the page and trying to find it again when you need it, Safari lets you leave the page open in a special section of the browser window called a *tab*. You can then use a second tab to visit your other sites, and to resume viewing the first site, you need only click its tab.

Open a Web Page in a Tab

Open a Link in a New Tab

1 Right-click the link you want to open.

2 Click **Open Link in New Tab**.

● A new tab appears with the page title.

3 Click the tab to display the page.

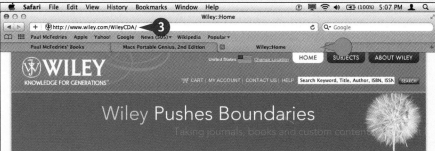

Create a New Tab

1 Click **File**.

2 Click **New Tab**.

● If you already have two or more tabs open, you can also click the **Create a new tab** icon (+).

● Safari creates a new tab.

3 Type the address of the page you want to load into the new tab.

4 Press Return.

● Safari displays the page in the tab.

Are there any shortcuts I can use to open web pages in tabs?

● Press and hold ⌘ and click a link to open the page in a tab.

● Press and hold ⌘ + Shift and click a link to open the page in a tab and display the tab.

● Type an address and then press ⌘ + Return to open the page in a new tab.

● Type an address and then press Shift + ⌘ + Return to open the page in a new foreground tab.

● Press Shift + ⌘ +] or Shift + ⌘ + [to cycle through the tabs.

● Press ⌘ + W to close the current tab.

● Press Option and click ⊠ to close every tab but the one you clicked.

Navigate Web Pages

After you have visited several pages, you can return to a page you visited earlier. Instead of retyping the address or looking for the link, Safari gives you some easier methods.

When you navigate from page to page, you create a kind of "path" through the web. Safari keeps track of this path by maintaining a list of the pages you have visited. You can use that list to go back to a page you have visited.

After you have gone back to a page you have visited, you can also use the same list of pages to go forward through the pages again.

Navigate Web Pages

Go Back One Page

1 Click the **Previous Page** icon (◄).

The previous page you visited appears.

Go Back Several Pages

1 Click and hold down on ◄.

Note: *The list of visited pages is different for each tab that you have open. If you do not see the page you want, you may need to click a different tab.*

A list of the pages you have visited appears.

2 Click the page you want to revisit.

The page appears.

Go Forward One Page

1 Click the **Next Page** icon (►).

The next page appears.

Note: *If you are at the last page viewed up to that point, ► is not active.*

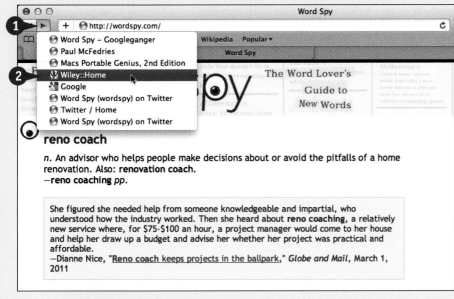

Go Forward Several Pages

1 Click and hold down ► on ►.

A list of the pages you have visited appears.

Note: *The list of visited pages is different for each tab that you have open. If you do not see the page you want, you may need to click a different tab.*

2 Click the page you want to revisit.

The page appears.

Are there any shortcuts I can use to navigate web pages?
Yes, there are a few useful keyboard shortcuts you can use:
- Press ⌘ + [to go back one page.
- Press ⌘ +] to go forward one page.
- Press Shift + ⌘ + H to return to the Safari home page (the first page you see when you open Safari).

Navigate with the History List

The Previous Page and Next Page buttons (◄ and ►) enable you to navigate pages in the current browser session. To redisplay sites that you have visited in the past few days or weeks, you need to use the History list, which is a collection of the websites and pages you have visited over the past month.

If you visit sensitive places such as an Internet banking site or your corporate site, you can increase security by clearing the history list so that other people cannot see where you have been.

Navigate with the History List

Load a Page from the History List

1. Click **History**.

2. Click the date when you visited the page.

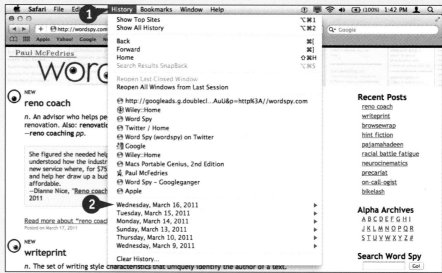

A submenu of pages that you visited during that day appears.

3. Click the page you want to revisit.

● The page appears.

Clear the History List

1 Click **History**.

2 Click **Clear History**.

Safari deletes all the pages from the history list.

Simplify It

Can I control the length of time that Safari keeps track of the pages I visit?

Yes, by following these steps:

1 In the menu bar, click **Safari**.

2 Click **Preferences**.

3 Click **General**.

4 In the Remove history items pop-up menu, click ⬩ and then click the amount of time you want Safari to track your history.

5 Click ●.

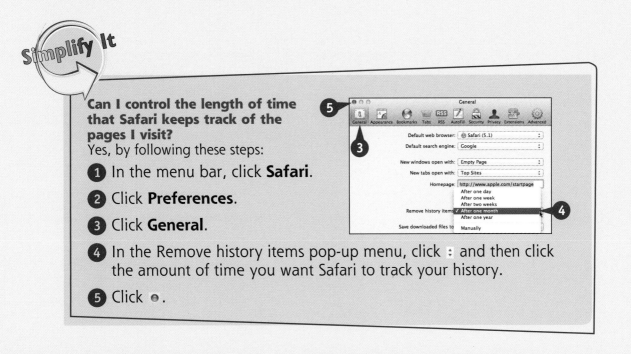

Change Your Home Page

Your home page is the web page that appears when you first start Safari. The default home page is usually the Apple.com Start page, but you can change that to any other page you want, or even to an empty page. This is useful if you do not use the Apple.com Start page, or if there is another page that you always visit at the start of your browsing session. For example, if you have your own website, it might make sense to always begin there.

Safari also comes with a command that enables you to view the home page at any time during your browsing session.

Change Your Home Page

Change the Home Page

1 Display the web page that you want to use as your home page.

2 Click **Safari**.

3 Click **Preferences**.

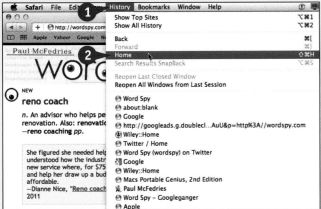

4 Click **General**.

5 Click **Set to Current Page**.

● Safari inserts the address of the current page in the Homepage text box.

Note: *If your Mac is not currently connected to the Internet, you can also type the new home page address manually using the Homepage text box.*

6 Click ●.

View the Home Page

1 Click **History**.

2 Click **Home**.

Note: *You can also display the home page by pressing* Shift + ⌘ + H.

Safari displays the home page.

Can I get Safari to open a new window without displaying the home page?
Yes, by following these steps:

1 In the menu bar, click **Safari**.

2 Click **Preferences**.

3 Click **General**.

4 In the New windows open with pop-up menu, click ⇕ and then click **Empty Page**.

5 Click ●.

Bookmark Web Pages

If you have web pages that you visit frequently, you can save yourself time by storing those pages as bookmarks within Safari. This enables you to display the pages with just a couple of mouse clicks.

The bookmark stores the name of the page as well as the address of the page. Most

bookmarks are stored on Safari's Bookmarks menu. However, Safari also offers the Bookmarks bar, which appears just below the address bar. You can put your favorite sites on the Bookmarks bar for easiest access.

Bookmark Web Pages

Bookmark a Web Page

1 Display the web page you want to save as a bookmark.

2 Click **Bookmarks**.

3 Click **Add Bookmark**.

● You can also run the Add Bookmark command by clicking **Add a bookmark** (+).

The Add Bookmark dialog appears.

Note: *You can also display the Add Bookmark dialog by pressing* ⌘ *+* D.

4 Edit the page name, if necessary.

5 Click ⌄ and then click the location where you want to store the bookmark.

6 Click **Add**.

Safari adds a bookmark for the page.

Display a Bookmarked Web Page

1 Click the **Show all bookmarks** button (📖).

● If you added the bookmark to the Bookmarks bar, click the page name.

● If you added the bookmark to a folder, click the folder and then click the page name.

The Bookmarks window appears.

2 Click ▶ to open the folder that contains the bookmark you want (▶ changes to ▼).

3 Double-click the bookmark.

The web page appears.

Simplify It

I use my Bookmarks bar a lot. Is there an easier way to display these pages?
Yes. Safari automatically assigns keyboard shortcuts to the first nine bookmarks, counting from left to right and not including folders. For example, you display the left-most bookmark by pressing ⌘ + 1. Moving to the right, the shortcuts are ⌘ + 2, ⌘ + 3, and so on.

How do I delete a bookmark?
If the site is on the Bookmarks bar, right-click the bookmark and then click **Delete**, or hold down ⌘ and drag it off the bar. For all other bookmarks, click 📖 to display the Bookmarks window. Locate the bookmark you want to remove, right-click the bookmark, and then click **Delete**. You can also click the bookmark and then press Del.

Search for Sites

If you need information on a specific topic, Safari has a built-in feature that enables you to quickly search the web for sites that have the information you require.

The web has a number of sites called *search engines* that enable you to find what you are looking for. By default, Safari uses the Google search site (www.google.com). Simple, one-word searches often return tens of thousands of *hits*, or matching sites. To improve your searching, type multiple search terms that define what you are looking for. To search for a phrase, enclose the words in quotation marks.

Search for Sites

1 Click in the search box.

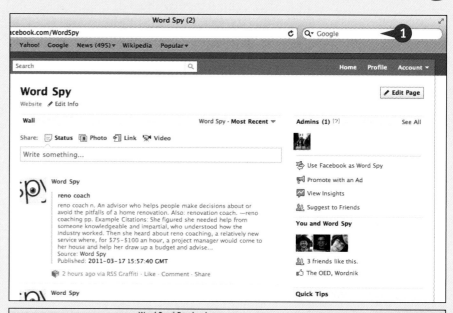

2 Type a word, phrase, or question that represents the information you want to find.

3 Press Return.

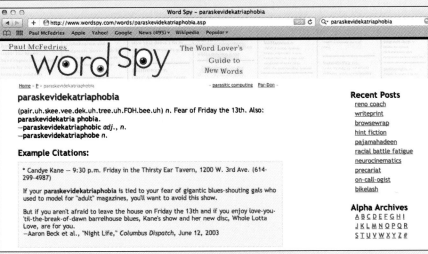

A list of pages that match your search text appears.

4 Click a web page.

The page appears.

Simplify It

Is there an easy way that I can rerun a recent search?
Yes, Safari maintains a list of the last few searches you ran. Follow these steps to quickly rerun one of those searches:

1 In the search box, click the **See your recent searches** icon (🔍▾).

2 Click the search you want to rerun.

In many cases you can also click the **Snapback** icon (⊙) to rerun the most recent search.

Safari sends the search text to Google again.

Chapter 4

Communicating via E-mail

Mac OS X comes with the Apple Mail application, which you can use to exchange e-mail messages with other people. Once you enter your e-mail account details into Mail, you can send e-mail to friends, family, colleagues, and even total strangers almost anywhere in the world. You can also attach documents, images, and other types of files to your e-mail messages, and you can set up a signature that adds text to an e-mail message automatically.

With Mail you can also read the messages that people send to you, reply to those messages, and forward those messages to other people.

Open and Close Mail

Mac OS X includes the Apple Mail application to enable you to use an e-mail account to exchange and manage e-mail messages. E-mail is one of the most popular Internet services because it offers three main advantages: It is universal, fast, and convenient.

E-mail is universal because nearly anyone who can access the Internet has an e-mail address. E-mail is fast because messages are generally delivered within a few minutes. E-mail is convenient because you can send messages at any time of day, and your recipient does not need to be at the computer or connected to the Internet.

Before you can send or receive e-mail messages, you must know how to start the Mail application.

Open and Close Mail

Open Mail

1 In the Dock, click the **Mail** icon (▨).

Note: If the Welcome to Mail dialog appears, see the next section to learn how to set up your first e-mail account in Mail.

The Mail window appears.

Close Mail

1 Click **Mail**.

2 Click **Quit Mail**.

Are there other methods I can use to open Mail?
If you have removed the icon from the Dock, there are a couple of other methods you can use to start Mail. If you have used Mail recently, click , click **Recent Items**, and then click **Safari**. You can also click **Spotlight** (), type **Mail**, and then click **Mail** in the search results.

Are there faster methods I can use to close Mail?
Probably the fastest method you can use to quit Mail is to right-click its icon () in the Dock and then click **Quit**. If your hands are closer to the keyboard than to the mouse, you can quit Mail by switching to the application and then pressing + .

Add an E-mail Account

Before you can send and receive e-mail messages, you must add your e-mail account to the Mail application. Your e-mail account is usually a POP (Post Office Protocol) account supplied by your Internet service provider, which should have supplied you with the POP account details. You can also set up web-based e-mail accounts with services such as Hotmail and Gmail. A web-based account is convenient because it enables you to send and receive messages from any computer.

If you have an Apple e-mail account, you can also set up Mail with your Apple account details.

Add an E-mail Account

Get Started Adding an Account

1 Click **File**.

2 Click **Add Account**.

Note: *If you are just starting Mail and the Welcome to Mail dialog is on-screen, you can skip Steps 1 and 2.*

The Add Account dialog appears. If you are starting Mail for the first time, the Welcome to Mail dialog is identical.

Add an Apple Account

1 Type your name.

2 Type your Apple account address.

3 Type your Apple account password.

4 Click **Create**.

Mail adds your Apple account.

Add a POP Account

1 Type your name.

2 Type your POP account address.

3 Type your POP account password and click **Continue**.

4 Click ↕ and then click **POP**.

5 Describe the account.

6 Type the address of the account's incoming mail server.

7 Edit the User Name text as required and click **Continue**.

8 Type a description of the outgoing mail server.

9 Type the address of the outgoing mail server.

● If your ISP requires authentication, click **Use Authentication** (☐ changes to ☑).

10 Click **Continue**, click **Continue** again, and then click **Create**.

Simplify It

My e-mail account requires me to use a nonstandard outgoing mail port. How do I set this up?

1 In the menu bar, click **Mail**.

2 Click **Preferences**.

3 Click **Accounts**.

4 In the Outgoing Mail Server (SMTP) list, click ↕ and then click **Edit SMTP Server List**.

5 Click the outgoing mail server.

6 Click **Advanced**.

7 Click **Use custom port** (○ changes to ⊙).

8 Type the nonstandard port number.

9 Click **OK**.

10 Click ●.

11 Click **Save**.

Send an E-mail Message

If you know the e-mail address of a person or organization, you can send an e-mail message to that address. An e-mail address is a set of characters that uniquely identifies the location of an Internet mailbox. Each e-mail address takes the form *username@domain*, where *username* is the name of the person's account with the ISP or within his or her organization, and *domain* is the Internet name of the company that provides the person's e-mail account.

When you send an e-mail message, it travels through your ISP's outgoing mail server. This server routes the messages to the recipient's incoming mail server, which then stores the message in the recipient's mailbox.

Send an E-mail Message

1 Click **New Message** (✐).

   Note: *You can also start a new message by pressing* ⌘ + N .

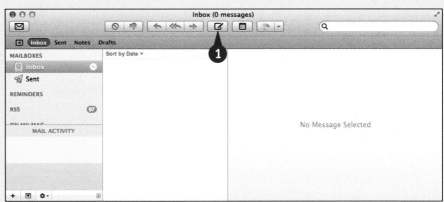

A message window appears.

2 Use the To field to type the e-mail address of the person to whom you are sending the message.

3 To send a copy of the message to another person, use the Cc field to type that person's e-mail address.

   Note: *You can add multiple e-mail addresses in both the To line and the Cc line. Separate each address with a comma (,).*

4 Use the Subject field to type a title or short description for the message.

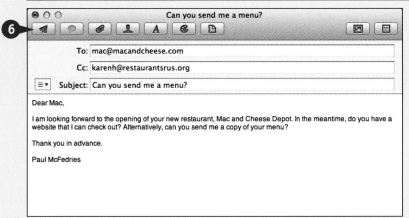

5 Type the message.

● To change the message font, click **Fonts** (A) to display the Font dialog.

● To change the text colors, click **Colors** (●) to display the Color Picker.

● To change the overall look of the message, click **Show Stationery** (▦) and then click a theme.

Note: *Unless you are sure your recipient's program supports formatting, it is best to send plain-text messages. To do this, click* **Format** *and then click* **Make Plain Text**.

6 Click **Send** (◢).

Mail sends your message.

Note: *Mail stores a copy of your message in the Sent folder.*

I have a large number of messages to compose. Do I have to be online to do this?

No, composing all the messages while you are offline is possible. Follow these steps:

❶ While disconnected from the Internet, start Mail.

❷ To ensure you are working offline, click **Mailbox**. If the Take All Accounts Offline command is enabled, click that command.

❸ Compose and send the message. Each time you click **Send** (◢), your message is stored temporarily in the Outbox folder.

❹ When you are done, connect to the Internet.

After a few moments, Mail automatically sends all the messages in the Outbox folder.

Add a File Attachment

If you have a document that you want to send to another person, you can attach the document to an e-mail message. A typical e-mail message is fine for short notes, but you may have something more complex to communicate, such as budget numbers or a slide show, or some form of media that you want to share, such as an image or a song.

Because these more complex types of data usually come in a separate file — such as a spreadsheet, presentation file, or picture file — it makes sense to send that file to your recipient. You do this by attaching the file to an e-mail message.

Add a File Attachment

1 Click **New Message** ( ).

A message window appears.

2 Fill in the recipients, subject, and message text as described in the previous section.

3 Press Return two or three times to move the cursor a few lines below your message.

4 Click **Attach** ( ).

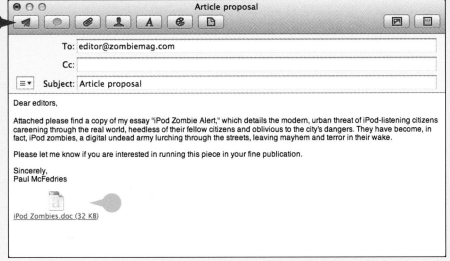

A file selection dialog appears.

5 Click the file you want to attach.

6 Click **Choose File**.

● Mail attaches the file to the message.

Note: *Another way to attach a file to a message is to click and drag the file from Finder and drop it inside the message.*

7 Repeat Steps **4** to **6** to attach additional files to the message.

8 Click **Send** (✈).

Mail sends your message.

Is there a limit to the number of files I can attach to a message?
The number of files you can attach to the message has no practical limit. However, you should be careful with the total *size* of the files you send. If you or the recipient has a slow Internet connection, sending or receiving the message can take an extremely long time. Also, many ISPs place a limit on the size of a message's attachments, which is usually between 2MB and 5MB. In general, use e-mail to send only a few small files at a time.

Add a Signature

In an e-mail message, a *signature* is a small amount of text that appears at the bottom of the message. Instead of typing this information manually in each message, you can save the signature in your Mail preferences. When you compose a new e-mail message, reply to an existing message, or forward a message, you can click a button to have Mail add the signature to your outgoing message.

Signatures usually contain personal contact information, such as your phone numbers, business address, and e-mail and website addresses. Mail supports multiple signatures, which is useful if you use Mail with multiple accounts or for different purposes such as business and personal.

Add a Signature

Create a Signature

1. Click **Mail**.
2. Click **Preferences**.

The Mail preferences appear.

3. Click **Signatures**.
4. Click the account for which you want to use the signature.
5. Click **Create a signature** (+).

   Mail adds a new signature.

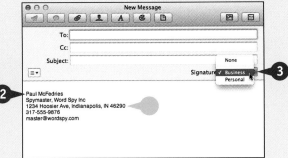

6 Type a name for the signature.

7 Type the signature text.

8 Repeat Steps **4** to **7** to add other signatures, if required.

   Note: *You can add as many signatures as you want. For example, you may want to have one signature for business use and another for personal use.*

9 Click ●.

Insert the Signature

1 Click **New Message** (✐) to start a new message.

2 In the message text area, move the insertion point to the location where you want the signature to appear.

3 Click ⬍ and then click the signature you want to insert.

● The signature appears in the message.

Simplify It

When I have multiple signatures, how can I choose which of them Mail adds automatically?

1 Follow Steps **1** to **4** to display the signature preferences and choose an account.

2 Click ⬍ and then click the signature you want to insert automatically into each message.

● If you prefer to add a signature manually, click **None** instead of a signature.

3 Click ●.

Receive and Read E-mail Messages

You must connect to your mail provider's incoming mail server to retrieve and read messages sent to you.

When another person sends you an e-mail message, that message ends up in your e-mail account's mailbox on the incoming mail server maintained by your ISP or e-mail provider. However, that company does not automatically pass along that message to you. Instead, you must use Mail to connect to your mailbox on the incoming mail server and then retrieve any messages waiting for you.

By default, Mail automatically checks for new messages every 5 minutes while you are online, but you can also check for new messages at any time.

Receive and Read E-mail Messages

Receive E-mail Messages

1 Click **Get Mail** (✉).

● The Mail Activity area lets you know if you have any incoming messages.

● If you have new messages, they appear in your Inbox folder with a blue dot in this column.

● The 🖂 icon in the Dock shows the number of unread messages in the Inbox folder.

Read a Message

1 Click the message.

2 Read the message text in the preview pane.

● If the message comes with an attached file, double-click the file icon to open it.

Note: *If you want to open the message in its own window, double-click the message.*

Simplify It

Can I change how often Mail automatically checks for messages?
Yes, by following these steps:

1 Click **Mail**.

2 Click **Preferences**.

The Mail preferences appear.

3 Click the **General** tab.

4 In the Check for new messages pop-up menu, click ⬦ and then click the time interval that you want Mail to use when checking for new messages automatically.

● If you do not want Mail to check for messages automatically, click **Manually** instead.

5 Click ⊙.

Reply to a Message

When a message you receive requires some kind of response — whether it is answering a question, supplying information, or providing comments — you can reply to that message.

Most replies go only to the person who sent the original message. However, it is also possible to send the reply to all the people who were included in the original message's To and Cc lines.

Mail includes the text of the original message in the reply, but you should edit the original message text to include only enough of the original message to put your reply into context.

Reply to a Message

1 Click the message to which you want to reply.

2 Click the reply type you want to use.

Click **Reply** (↩) to respond only to the person who sent the message.

Click **Reply All** (↩) to respond to all the addresses in the message's From, To, and Cc lines.

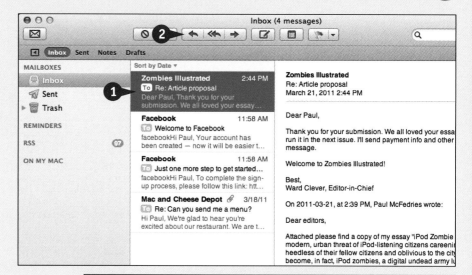

A message window appears.

● Mail automatically inserts the recipient addresses.

● Mail also inserts the subject line, preceded by Re:.

● Mail includes the original message text at the bottom of the reply.

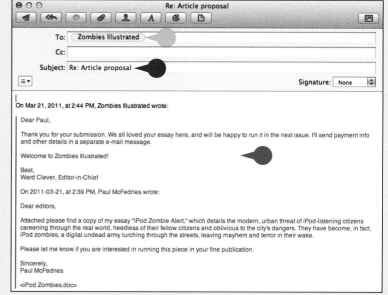

Re: Article proposal

To: Zombies Illustrated

Cc:

Subject: Re: Article proposal

Signature: None

On Mar 21, 2011, at 2:44 PM, Zombies Illustrated wrote:

Dear Paul,

Thank you for your submission. We all loved your essay here, and will be happy to run it in the next issue. I'll send payment info and other details in a separate e-mail message.

Welcome to Zombies Illustrated!

Best,
Ward Clever, Editor-in-Chief

③ Edit the original message to include only the text relevant to your reply.

Re: Article proposal

To: Zombies Illustrated

Cc:

Subject: Re: Article proposal

Signature: None

Hello Ward,

Thank you very much for accepting my essay. I'm looking forward to being part of the ZI team! ④

Cheers,
Paul

On Mar 21, 2011, at 2:44 PM, Zombies Illustrated wrote:

Dear Paul,

Thank you for your submission. We all loved your essay here, and will be happy to run it in the next issue. I'll send payment info and other details in a separate e-mail message.

Welcome to Zombies Illustrated!

Best,
Ward Clever, Editor-in-Chief

④ Click the area above the original message text and type your reply.

⑤ Click **Send** ( ).

Mail sends your reply.

Note: *Mail stores a copy of your reply in the Sent folder.*

Simplify It

I received a message inadvertently. Is there a way that I can pass it along to the correct recipient?
Yes. Click the message that you received inadvertently, click **Message**, and then click **Redirect** (or press Shift + ⌘ + E). Type the recipient's address and then click **Send**. Replies to this message will be sent to the original sender, not to you.

How much of the original message should I include in my reply?
If the original message is fairly short, you usually do not need to edit the text. However, if the original message is long, and your response deals only with part of that message, you will save the recipient time and confusion by deleting everything except the relevant portion of the text.

Forward a Message

If a message has information relevant to or that concerns another person, you can forward a copy of the message to that person. You can also include your own comments in the forward. In the body of the forward, Mail includes the original message's addresses, date, and subject line. Below this information Mail also includes the text of the original message. In most cases you will leave the entire message intact so your recipient can see it. However, if only part of the message is relevant to the recipient, you should edit the original message accordingly.

Forward a Message

1. Click the message that you want to forward.

2. Click **Forward** (→).

   Note: You can also press Shift + ⌘ + F.

A message window appears.

● Mail inserts the subject line, preceded by Fwd:.

● The original message's addressees (To and From), date, subject, and text are included at the top of the forward.

3. Type the e-mail address of the person to whom you are forwarding the message.

4. To send a copy of the forward to another person, type that person's e-mail address in the Cc line.

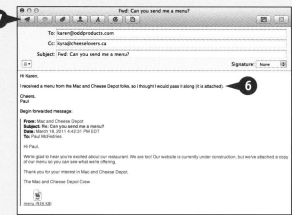

⑤ Edit the original message to include only the text relevant to your forward.

⑥ Click the area above the original message text and type your comments.

⑦ Click **Send** ( ).

Mail sends your forward.

Note: *Mail stores a copy of your forward in the Sent folder.*

Note: *You can forward someone a copy of the actual message instead of just a copy of the message text. Click the message, click **Message**, and then click **Forward As Attachment***. *Mail creates a new message and includes the original message as an attachment.*

Simplify It

Mail always formats my replies as rich text, even when the original message is plain text. How can I fix this problem?
You can configure Mail to always reply using the same format as the original message. Follow these steps:

① Click **Mail**.

② Click **Preferences**.

The Mail preferences appear.

③ Click the **Composing** tab.

④ Click the **Use the same message format as the original message** check box (☐ changes to ☑).

⑤ Click ●.

Chapter 5

Tracking Your Contacts and Events

Mac OS X comes with two applications that can help you manage your busy life. You use the Address Book application to manage your contacts — your friends, family, colleagues, and clients — by storing information such as phone numbers, e-mail addresses, and street addresses.

You use the iCal application to enter and track events such as appointments, meetings, birthdays, and trips. iCal not only stores the time and place for each event, but can also remind you when an event occurs so you will never miss an appointment.

Open and Close Address Book

Mac OS X includes the Address Book application to enable you to manage information about the people you know, whether they are colleagues, friends, or family members. Address Book refers to these people as *contacts*, and you store each person's data in an object called a *card*.

Before you can add or work with contacts, you must know how to start the Address Book application. When you are finished with Address Book, you should close it to reduce desktop clutter and save system resources.

Open and Close Address Book

Open Address Book

1 In the Dock, click **Address Book** (□).

The Address Book window appears.

Close Address Book

1 Click **Address Book**.

2 Click **Quit Address Book**.

Are there other methods I can use to open Address Book?
If you have removed the ⬜ icon from the Dock, there are a couple of other methods you can use. If you have used Address Book recently, click , click **Recent Items**, and then click **Address Book**. You can also click **Spotlight** (🔍), type **Address**, and then click **Address Book** in the search results.

Are there faster methods I can use to close Address Book?
Probably the fastest method you can use to quit Address Book is to right-click its icon (⬜) and then click **Quit**. If your hands are closer to the keyboard than to the mouse, you can quit Address Book by switching to the application and then pressing ⌘ + Q.

Add a New Contact

To store contact information for a particular person, you first need to create a new contact within Address Book. You do that by creating a new card, which is an Address Book item that stores data about a person or company.

Each card can store a wide variety of information. For example, you can store a person's name, company name, phone numbers, e-mail address and instant messaging data, street address, notes, and much more.

Although you will mostly use Address Book cards to store data about people, you can also use a card to keep information about companies.

1 Click **File**.

2 Click **New Card**.

● You can also begin a new contact by clicking + .

> **Note:** *You can also run the New Card command by pressing ⌘ + N.*

● Address Book adds a new card.

3 Use the First field to type the contact's first name.

4 Use the Last field to type the contact's last name.

5 Use the Company field to type the contact's company name.

6 If the contact is a company, click **Company** (☐ changes to ☑).

⑦ In the first Phone field, click ⬍ and then click the category you want to use.

⑧ Type the phone number.

⑨ Repeat Steps **7** and **8** to enter data in some or all of the other fields.

Note: See the next section to learn how to add more fields to the card.

⑩ Click **Done**.

Address Book saves the new card.

Simplify It

If I include a contact's e-mail address, is there a way to send that person a message without having to type the address?

① Click the contact's card.

② Click the e-mail address category.

③ Click **Send Email**.

Apple Mail displays a new e-mail message with the contact already added in the To line.

④ Fill in the rest of the message as required.

⑤ Click **Send**.

Note: Alternatively, start a new message in Mail, click **Address**, click the contact, and then click **To:** (or **Cc:** or **Bcc:**).

Edit a Contact

If you need to make changes to the information already in a contact's card, or if you need to add new information to a card, you can edit the card from within Address Book.

The default fields you see in a card are not the only types of data you can store for a contact.

Address Book offers a large number of extra fields. These include useful fields such as Middle Name, Nickname, Job Title, Department, URL (web address), and Birthday. You can also add extra fields for common data items such as phone numbers, e-mail addresses, and dates.

Edit a Contact

① Click the card you want to edit.

② Click **Edit**.

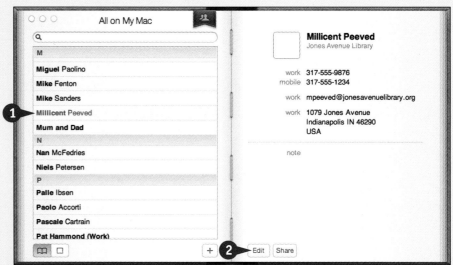

● Address Book makes the card's fields available for editing.

③ Edit the existing fields as required.

④ To add a field, click an empty placeholder and then type the field data.

⑤ To remove a field, click ⊖.

6 To add a new field type, click **Card**.

7 Click **Add Field**.

8 Click the type of field you want.

● Address Book adds the field to the card.

9 When you have completed your edits, click **Done**.

Address Book saves the edited card.

Simplify It

How do I add a picture for the new contact?

1 Click the contact's card.

2 Click **Edit**.

3 Double-click the picture box.

4 Click **Choose** and choose the picture you want to use.

5 Click **Open**.

6 Click and drag the picture to the position you want.

7 Click **Set**.

8 Click **Done**.

Create a Contact Group

You can organize your contacts into one or more groups, which is useful if you want to view just a subset of your contacts. For example, you could create separate groups for friends, family members, work colleagues, or business clients.

Groups are particularly handy if you have a large number of contacts in Address Book. By creating and maintaining groups, you can navigate your contacts more easily. You can also perform groupwide tasks, such as sending a single e-mail message to everyone in the group.

You can create a group first and then add members, or you can select members in advance and then create the group.

Create a Contact Group

1 Click **File**.

2 Click **New Group**.

Note: You can also run the New Group command by pressing Shift + ⌘ + N.

● Address Book adds a new group.

3 Type a name for the group.

4 Press Return.

5 Click **All on My Mac**.

6 Click and drag a contact to the group.

Address Book adds the contact to the group.

7 Repeat Step **6** for the other contacts you want to add to the group.

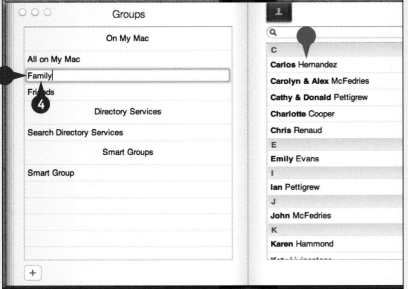

Create a Group of Selected Contacts

1 Select the contacts you want to include in the new group.

Note: *To select multiple contacts, press and hold ⌘ and click each card.*

2 Click **File**.

3 Click **New Group From Selection**.

● Address Book adds a new group.

● Address Book adds the selected contacts as group members.

4 Type a name for the group.

5 Press Return.

Can I send an e-mail message to the group?

Yes, this is one of the best reasons to create a group because you can send a single message to the group, and Mail automatically sends a copy to each member of the group. Right-click the group and then click **Send Email to "*Group*"**, where *Group* is the name of the group.

What is a smart group?

This is a special group where each member has some data in common, such as the company name. To create a smart group, click **File**, and then click **New Smart Group**. Now specify one or more criteria that define the group, and Address Book automatically adds members to the group if they meet those criteria.

Open and Close iCal

Your Mac comes with the iCal application to enable you to manage your schedule. iCal enables you to create and work with events, which are either scheduled appointments such as meetings, lunches, or visits to the dentist; or all-day activities, such as birthdays, anniversaries, or vacations. You can also use iCal to keep track of to-do items, which are tasks that you have to perform.

Before you can add or work with events (appointments, meetings, all-day activities, and so on), and to-do items (tasks), you must know how to start the iCal application.

Open and Close iCal

Open iCal

1 In the Dock, click **iCal** ().

The iCal window appears.

Close iCal

1 Click **iCal**.

2 Click **Quit iCal**.

Are there other methods I can use to open iCal?
If you have removed the ⬛ icon from the Dock, there are a couple of other methods you can use. If you have used iCal recently, click ⬛, click **Recent Items**, and then click **iCal**. You can also click **Spotlight** (⬛), type **ical**, and then click **iCal** in the search results.

Are there faster methods I can use to close iCal?
Probably the fastest method you can use to quit iCal is to right-click its icon (⬛) and then click **Quit**. If your hands are closer to the keyboard than to the mouse, you can quit iCal by switching to the application and pressing ⬛ + ⬛.

Navigate the Calendar

Before you create an event such as an appointment or meeting, or an all-day event such as a conference or trip, you must first select the date on which the event occurs. You do that in iCal by navigating the built-in calendar or by specifying the date you want.

iCal also lets you change the calendar view to suit your needs. For example, you can show just a single day's worth of events if you want to concentrate on that day's activities. Similarly, you can view a week's worth of events if you want to get a larger sense of what your overall schedule looks like.

Navigate the Calendar

Use the Calendar

1 Click **Month**.

2 Click the **Next** button (▶) until the month of your event appears.

● If you go too far, click the **Previous** button (◀) to move back to the month you want.

● To see a specific date, click the day and then click **Day** (or press ⌘ + ①).

● To see a specific week, click any day within the week and then click **Week** (or press ⌘ + ②).

● To return to viewing the entire month, click **Month** (or press ⌘ + ③).

● If you want to return to today's date, click **Today** (or press ⌘ + ⊤).

Go to a Specific Date

1 Click **View**.

2 Click **Go to Date**.

Note: You can also select the Go to Date command by pressing Shift + ⌘ + T.

The Go to date dialog appears.

3 Use the Date text box to type the date you want using the format mm/dd/yyyy.

● You can also click the day, month, or year and then click 〼 to increase or decrease the value.

4 Click **Show**.

5 Click **Day**.

● iCal displays the date.

In the Week view, the week begins on Sunday. How can I change this to Monday?
iCal's default Week view has Sunday on the left and Saturday on the right. Many people prefer to display the weekend days together, with Monday on the left signaling the start of the week. To set this up, follow these steps:

1 Click **iCal** in the menu bar.

2 Click **Preferences**.

3 Click the **General** tab.

4 In the Start week on pop-up menu, click 〼 and then click **Monday**.

5 Click ●.

Create an Event

You can help organize your life by using iCal to record your events — such as appointments, meetings, phone calls, and dates — on the date and time they occur.

If the event has a set time and duration — for example, a meeting or a lunch date — you add

the event directly to the calendar as a regular appointment. If the event has no set time — for example, a birthday, anniversary, or multiple-day event such as a convention or vacation — you can create an all-day event.

Create an Event

Create a Regular Event

1 Navigate to the date when the event occurs.

2 Click **Calendars**.

3 Click the calendar you want to use.

4 Double-click the time when the event starts.

● iCal adds a one-hour event.

> **Note:** If the event is less than or more than an hour, you can also click and drag the mouse (↖) over the full event period.

5 Type the name of the event.

6 Press Return.

Create an All-Day Event

1. Click **Week**.

2. Navigate to the week that includes the date when the event occurs.

3. Click **Calendars**.

4. Click the calendar you want to use.

5. Double-click anywhere inside the event date's all-day section.

● iCal adds a new all-day event.

6. Type the name of the event.

7. Press [Return].

Simplify It

How can I specify event details such as the location and a reminder message?

1. Follow the steps in this section to create an event.

2. Double-click the event.

3. Click **Edit**.

4. Use the location text box to type the location of the event.

5. Use the alert pop-up menu to choose **Message**.

6. Choose the amount of time before the event that you want to receive the reminder.

7. Click **Done**.

   iCal saves the new event configuration.

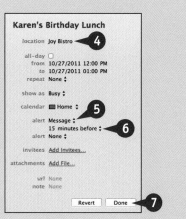

Create a Repeating Event

If you have an activity or event that recurs at a regular interval, you can create an event and configure it to automatically repeat in iCal. This saves you from having to repeatedly add the future events yourself because iCal adds them for you automatically.

You can repeat an event daily, weekly, monthly, or yearly. For even greater flexibility, you can set up a custom interval. For example, you could have an event repeat every five days, every second Friday, on the first Monday of every month, and so on.

Create a Repeating Event

① Follow the steps in the previous section to create an event.

② Double-click the event.

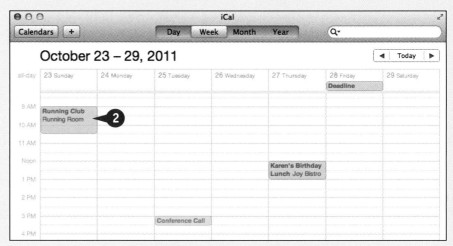

iCal displays information for the event.

③ Click **Edit**.

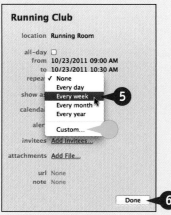

iCal opens the event for editing.

4 Beside the repeat label, click **None**.

5 Click the interval you want to use.

● If you want to specify a custom interval such as every two weeks or the first Monday of every month, click **Custom** and configure your interval in the dialog that appears.

6 Click **Done**.

iCal adds the repeating events to the calendar.

Simplify It

How do I configure an event to stop after a certain number of occurrences?

1 Follow Steps **1** to **5** to select a recurrence interval.

2 Beside the end label, click **None** and then click **After**.

3 Type the number of occurrences you want.

4 Click **Done**.

Is it possible to delete just a single occurrence out of a recurring series of events?
Yes, you can delete one occurrence from the calendar without affecting the rest of the series. Click the occurrence you want to delete, and then press Del. iCal asks whether you want to delete all the occurrences or just the selected occurrence. Click **Delete Only This Event**.

Chapter 6

Playing and Organizing Music

Using iTunes, you can create a library of music, either by importing tracks from a music CD or by purchasing music from the online iTunes store. You can then use that library to play songs or albums, organize your music by genre, and create custom collections of songs called playlists. You can also use iTunes to burn songs or playlists to a recordable CD, listen to music CDs, and manage music on an iPod, iPad, or iPhone.

This chapter shows you how to perform many of these tasks, and it also introduces you to iTunes and the features of the iTunes window.

Open and Close iTunes

Your Mac includes iTunes to enable you to play back and manage various types of audio files. iTunes also includes features for playing videos, watching movies and TV shows, and organizing eBooks, but this chapter focuses on iTunes's audio features.

To begin using the program, you must first learn how to find and open the iTunes window. When you finish using the program, you can close the iTunes window to free up computer processing power.

Open and Close iTunes

Open iTunes

① In the Dock, click **iTunes** ( ).

The iTunes window appears.

Close iTunes

1 Click **iTunes**.

2 Click **Quit iTunes**.

Are there other methods I can use to open iTunes?
If you have removed the 🎵 icon from the Dock, there are a couple of other methods you can use. If you have used iTunes recently, click the Apple icon (), click **Recent Items**, and then click **iTunes**. You can also click **Spotlight** (🔍), type **itunes**, and then click **iTunes** in the search results.

Are there faster methods I can use to close iTunes?
Probably the fastest method you can use to quit iTunes is to click **Close** (). Alternatively, right-click the iTunes icon () and then click **Quit**. Finally, if your hands are closer to the keyboard than to the mouse, you can quit iTunes by switching to the application and then pressing ⌘ + Q.

Understanding the iTunes Library

Most of your iTunes time will be spent in the Library, so you need to understand what the Library is and how you work with it. In particular, you need to understand the various categories — such as music and audiobooks — that iTunes uses to organize the Library's audio content. Also, to make it easier to navigate the Library, you need to know how to configure the Library to show only the categories that you'll be working with.

The iTunes Library

The iTunes Library is where your Mac stores the files that you can play and work with in the iTunes application. Although iTunes has some video components, its focus is on audio features, so most of the Library sections are audio related. These sections enable you to work with music, podcasts, audiobooks, ringtones, and Internet radio.

Understanding Library Categories

The left side of the iTunes window is called the Source List and it displays the various categories that are available in the iTunes Library. In the Library list, the audio-related categories include Music, Podcasts, Books (for audiobooks), Ringtones, and Radio. The Store list includes items you've purchased from the iTunes Store.

Each category shows you the contents of that category and the details for each item. For example, in the Music category, you can see details such as the name of each album and the artist who recorded it.

Configuring the Library

You can configure which categories of the iTunes Library appear in the Library list on the left side of the iTunes window. Click **iTunes** and then click **Preferences** to open the iTunes preferences, and then click the **General** tab. In the Show section, click the check box for each type of content you want to work with (☐ changes to ☑), and then click **OK**.

Navigate the iTunes Window

Familiarizing yourself with the various elements of the iTunes window is a good idea so that you can easily navigate and activate elements when you are ready to play audio files, music CDs, or podcasts; import and burn audio CDs; create your own playlists; or listen to Internet radio.

In particular, you need to learn the iTunes playback controls because you will use them to control the playback of almost all music you work with in iTunes. It is also worthwhile learning the different View options because these often come in handy when navigating the iTunes Library.

Playback Controls

These buttons control media playback and enable you to adjust the volume.

Sort Buttons

These buttons sort the contents of the current iTunes category.

Status Area

This area displays information about the item that is currently playing or the action that iTunes is currently performing.

View Options

These buttons control how the contents of the current category appear. Click **List** (≡) to view the contents as a list by song; click **Album List** (≣) to view the contents as a list by album; click **Grid** (⠿) to view the contents as thumbnails; click **Cover Flow** (▦) to view the contents as scrolling thumbnails.

Categories

This area displays the iTunes Library categories that you can view.

Contents

The contents of the current iTunes Library source appear here.

Genius Sidebar

This area displays a list of songs, albums, or other iTunes Store content similar to the current item in the Library.

Play a Song

You use the Music category of the iTunes Library to play a song that is stored on your computer. Although iTunes offers several methods to locate the song you want to play, the easiest method is to display the albums you have in your iTunes Library, and then open the album that contains the song you want to play.

While the song is playing, you can control the volume to suit the music or your current location. If you need to leave the room or take a call, you can also pause the currently playing song.

Play a Song

① Click **Music**.

② Click **Albums**.

③ Double-click the album that contains the song you want to play.

● If you want to play the entire album, click **Play Album**.

④ Click the song you want to play.

⑤ Click the **Play** button (▶).

iTunes begins playing the song.

● Information about the song playback appears here.

● iTunes displays a speaker icon (🔊) beside the currently playing song.

● If you need to stop the song temporarily, click the **Pause** button (⏸).

Note: *You can also pause and restart a song by pressing the* Spacebar.

● You can use the Volume slider to adjust the volume (see the tip, below).

Note: *See the "Play a Music CD" section to learn more about the playback buttons.*

Simplify It

How do I adjust the volume?

To turn the volume up or down, click and drag the **Volume** slider to the left (to reduce the volume) or to the right (to increase the volume). You can also press ⌘ + ⬇ to reduce the volume, or ⌘ + ⬆ to increase the volume.

To mute the volume, either drag the **Volume** slider all the way to the left, or press Option + ⌘ + ⬇. To restore the volume, adjust the **Volume** slider or press Option + ⌘ + ⬇.

Play a Music CD

You can play your favorite music CDs in iTunes. When you insert an audio disc in your Mac's optical drive (that is, a drive capable of reading CDs and DVDs), the CD appears in the Devices section of the iTunes Library. When you click the CD, the iTunes contents area displays the individual tracks on the CD, and if you have an Internet connection you see the name of each track as well as other track data. During playback, you can skip tracks and pause and resume play.

To play a music CD, your Mac must have an optical drive.

Play a Music CD

Play a CD

1 Insert a music CD into your Mac's optical drive.

● The music CD appears in iTune's Devices category.

iTunes asks if you want to import the CD.

2 Click **No**.

Note: *To learn how to import a CD, see the section "Import Tracks from a Music CD."*

● If you have an Internet connection, iTunes shows the contents of the CD.

Note: *iTunes shows the contents for most CDs, but it may not show the correct information for some discs, particularly noncommercial mixed CDs.*

3 Click ▶.

iTunes begins playing the CD from the first track.

Skip a Track

4 Click the **Next** button (⏭) to skip to the next track.

Note: You can also skip to the next track by pressing ⌘ + ➡.

5 Click the **Previous** button (⏮) to skip to the beginning of the current track; click ⏮ again to skip to the previous track.

Note: You can also skip to the previous track by pressing ⌘ + ⬅.

Pause and Resume Play

6 Click ⏸ (⏸ changes to ▶).

iTunes pauses playback.

7 Click ▶.

iTunes resumes playback where you left off.

Simplify It

Can I change the CD's audio levels?
Yes, iTunes has a graphic equalizer component that you can use to adjust the levels. To display the equalizer, click **Window** and then click **Equalizer** (or press Option + ⌘ + 2). In the Equalizer window, use the sliders to set the audio levels, or click the pop-up menu (⬍) to choose an audio preset.

Can I display visualizations during playback?
Yes. You can click **View** and then click **Show Visualizer** (you can also press ⌘ + T). To change the currently displayed visualizer, click **View**, click **Visualizer**, and then click the visualization you want to view.

continued

Play a Music CD *(continued)*

iTunes gives you more options for controlling the CD playback. For example, you can easily switch from one song to another on the CD. You can also use the Repeat feature to tell iTunes to start the CD over from the beginning after it has finished playing the CD. iTunes also offers the Shuffle feature, which tells iTunes to play the CD's tracks in random order.

When the CD is done, you can use iTunes to eject it from your Mac.

If you want to learn how to import music from the CD to iTunes, see the section "Import Tracks from a Music CD."

Play a Music CD *(continued)*

Play Another Song

8 In the list of songs, double-click the song you want to play.

iTunes begins playing the song.

Repeat the CD

9 Click the **Repeat** button (⟲ changes to ⟲).

iTunes restarts the CD after the last track finishes playing.

To repeat just the current song, click ⟲ again (⟲ changes to ⟲).

Play Songs Randomly

10 Click the **Shuffle** button (⇄ changes to ⇄).

iTunes shuffles the order of play.

Eject the CD

11 Click the **Eject** button (⏏) beside the CD.

Note: *You can also eject the CD by pressing and holding the ⏏ key on the keyboard.*

iTunes ejects the CD from your Mac's CD or DVD drive.

Why do I not see the song titles after I insert my music CD?
When you play a music CD, iTunes tries to gather information about the album from the Internet. If you still see only track numbers, it may be that you do not have an Internet connection established or that you inserted a noncommercial, mixed CD. Connect to the Internet, click **Advanced**, and then click **Get CD Track Names**.

Import Tracks from a Music CD

You can add tracks from a music CD to the iTunes Library. This enables you to listen to an album without having to put the CD into your Mac's optical drive each time. The process of adding tracks from a CD is called *importing*, or *ripping*, in Mac OS X.

After you import the tracks from a music CD, you can play those tracks from the Music category of the iTunes Library. You can also use the tracks to create your own playlists and to create your own custom CDs.

Import Tracks from a Music CD

① Insert a CD into your Mac's CD or DVD drive.

● The music CD appears in iTune's Devices category.

iTunes asks if you want to import the CD.

② Click **No**.

● If you want to import the entire CD, click **Yes** and skip the rest of the steps in this section.

● iTunes shows the contents of the CD.

③ Click the check box so it is unchecked next to each CD track that you do not want to copy (☑ changes to ☐).

④ Click **Import CD**.

iTunes begins importing the check-marked track or tracks.

● This area displays the copy progress for each track.

● When iTunes is importing a track, it displays ⊗ beside the track number.

● When iTunes is finished importing a track, it displays ⊘ beside the track number.

● When iTunes has completed the import, you see ⊘ beside the track numbers of all the tracks you selected.

5 Click the **Eject** button (⏏) beside the CD, or press ⏏.

*Note: To delete an imported track, click the **Music** category, open the album you imported, right-click the track that you want to remove, and then click **Delete**.*

Simplify It

Can I specify a different quality when importing?
Yes. You do that by changing the *bit rate*, which is a measure of how much of the CD's original data gets copied to your computer. This is measured in kilobits per second (Kbps): The higher the value, the higher the quality, but the more disk space each track takes up. Click **Import Settings** to open the Import Settings dialog. In the Settings pop-up menu, click ↕, click **Custom**, and then use the Stereo Bit Rate pop-up to click the value you want.

Create a Playlist

A *playlist* is a collection of songs that are related in some way. Using your iTunes Library, you can create customized playlists that include only the songs that you want to hear.

For example, you might want to create a playlist of upbeat or festive songs to play during a party or celebration. Similarly, you might want to create a playlist of your current favorite songs to burn to a CD.

Create a Playlist

Create the Playlist

1 Click **File**.

2 Click **New Playlist**.

   Note: *You can also choose the New Playlist command by pressing ⌘ + N.*

● iTunes creates a new playlist.

3 Type a name for the new playlist.

4 Press Return.

Add Songs to the Playlist

1 Click **Music**.

2 Open an album that has one or more songs you want to add to the playlist.

3 Click a song that you want to add to the new playlist.

Note: *If the album has multiple songs you want in the playlist, hold down ⌘ and click each of songs you want to add.*

4 Drag the selected track (or tracks) and drop them on your playlist.

5 Repeat Steps **2** to **4** to add more songs to the playlist.

6 Click the playlist.

● iTunes displays the songs you added to the playlist.

● If you want to listen to the playlist, click ▷.

Simplify It

Is there a faster way to create and populate a playlist?

Click **Music** to open the Music category of the iTunes Library. Press and hold the ⌘ key and then click each song that you want to include in your playlist. Click **File** and then click **New Playlist from Selection** (or press `Shift` + `⌘` + `N`). Type the new playlist name and then press `Return`.

Is there any way to make iTunes add songs to a playlist automatically?

You can create a *smart playlist* that includes songs that have one or more properties in common, such as the genre or rating. Click **File** and then click **New Smart Playlist** (or press `Option` + `⌘` + `N`). Use the Smart Playlist dialog to create one or more rules that define which songs you want to appear in the playlist.

Burn Music Files to a CD

You can copy, or *burn*, music files from your Mac onto a CD. Burning CDs is a great way to create customized CDs that you can listen to on the computer or in a portable device that plays CDs.

You can burn music files from within the iTunes window. The easiest way to do this is to create a playlist of the songs you want to burn to the CD. You then organize the playlist by sorting the tracks in the order you want to hear them.

To burn music files to a CD, your Mac must have a recordable optical drive.

Burn Music Files to a CD

1 Insert a blank CD into your Mac's recordable disc drive.

2 If you already have iTunes running and your Mac asks you to choose an action, click **Ignore**.

● If you do not yet have iTunes running, use the Action menu to click ⁝, click **Open iTunes**, and then click **OK**.

3 Create a playlist for the songs you want to burn to the disc.

   Note: See the section "Create a Playlist" to learn how to build an iTunes playlist.

4 Click the playlist that you want to burn.

5 To modify the play order, click and drag a song and drop it on a new position in the playlist.

6 Repeat Step 5 to get the songs in the order in which you want them to appear on the CD.

7 Click **File**.

8 Click **Burn Playlist to Disc**.

The Burn Settings dialog appears.

9 Click **Burn**.

iTunes burns the songs to the CD.

Can I control the interval between songs on the CD?
Yes. By default, iTunes adds 2 seconds between each track on the CD. You can change that in the Burn Settings dialog. In the Gap Between Songs pop-up menu, click :, and then click the interval you want to use: None, or any time between 1 second and 5 seconds.

What happens if I have more music than can fit on a single disc?
You can still add all the music you want to burn to the playlist. iTunes fills the first disc and then adds the remaining songs to a second disc. After iTunes finishes burning the first disc, it prompts you to insert the next one.

Purchase Music from the iTunes Store

You can add music to your iTunes Library by purchasing songs or albums from the iTunes Store. iTunes downloads the song or album to your computer and then adds it to both the Music category and the Purchased playlist. You can then play and manage the song or album just like any other content in the iTunes Library.

To purchase music from the iTunes Store, you must have an Apple account. This can either be an account on the Apple Store site or an Apple account. You can also use an AOL account, if you have one.

Purchase Music from the iTunes Store

1 Click **iTunes Store**.

2 Click **Music**.

The iTunes Store appears.

3 Locate the music you want to purchase.

● You can use the Search box to search for an artist, album, or song.

4 Click **Buy Album**.

● If you want to purchase just a song, click the song's **Buy** button instead.

iTunes asks you to sign in to your iTunes store account.

⑤ If you have not signed in to your account, you must type your password.

⑥ Click **Buy**.

iTunes asks you to confirm your purchase.

⑦ Click **Buy**.

iTunes charges your credit card and begins downloading the music to your Mac.

● To watch the progress of the download, click **Downloads**.

Can I use my purchased music on other computers and devices?
Although many iTunes Store media — particularly movies and TV shows — have digital rights management (DRM) restrictions applied to prevent illegal copying, the songs and albums in the iTunes Store are DRM free. You can play them on multiple computers and media devices (such as iPods, iPads, and iPhones), and burn them to multiple CDs.

If I want to purchase a number of songs, how do I avoid having many $0.99 charges on my credit card bill?
To avoid many small iTunes charges, purchase an iTunes gift card. On the back of the card, scratch off the sticker that covers the redeem code. In iTunes, access the iTunes Store and click **Redeem** at the bottom of the store. Type in the redeem code, and then click **Redeem**.

Chapter 7

Synchronizing an iPod, iPhone, or iPad

If you have an iPod — including an iPod Classic, iPod touch, iPod Nano, or iPod Shuffle — an iPhone, or an iPad, you can connect it to your Mac and keep the data on the two devices in sync.

This chapter shows you how to connect an iPod, iPhone, or iPad to your Mac. With the connection in place, you then learn how to synchronize various media, including music, photos, movies, and TV shows. You also learn how to

synchronize photos from an iPhone or iPad to your Mac. This chapter also shows you how to synchronize e-mail accounts, contacts, calendars, and apps.

Connect an iPod, iPhone, or iPad

Before you can synchronize data between Mac OS X and your iPod, iPhone, or iPad, you need to connect the device to your Mac.

To connect an iPod, iPhone, or iPad, you need the USB cable that came as part of the device package. You will connect one end of that cable to your Mac, so you need to make sure that your Mac has a free USB port for the connection. You can also connect an iPod, iPhone, or iPad using an optional dock.

Connect an iPod, iPhone, or iPad

Connect the iPod, iPhone, or iPad

1 Using the device cable, attach the USB connector to a free USB port on your Mac.

2 Attach the other end of the cable to the port on the device or dock.

Mac OS X launches iTunes and automatically begins synchronizing the device.

Note: *Mac OS X usually also launches iPhoto to synchronize photos from the iPhone or iPad. See the section "Synchronize Photos from Your Device." For now, either quit iPhoto or switch to iTunes.*

Disconnect the iPod, iPhone, or iPad

1 In iTunes, click the eject button (⏏) beside your device's name.

iTunes begins releasing the iPod.

Note: See the following tip to learn when it is safe to disconnect the cable from an iPod.

2 Pinch the sides of the connector and then pull the connector away from the device.

3 Disconnect the cable from the Mac's USB port.

Note: If your Mac has two or more free USB ports and you synchronize your device frequently, consider leaving the cable plugged into a USB port for easier connections in the future.

Is there a way to prevent iTunes from starting the synchronization automatically when I connect my device?
Yes. In iTunes, click **iTunes** and then click **Preferences** to open the iTunes preferences window. Click the **Devices** tab and then click the **Prevent iPods, iPhones, and iPads from syncing automatically** check box (☐ changes to ☑). Click **OK**.

Do I always have to eject my iPod before disconnecting it?
No, not always. You must first eject the iPod if the iPod screen says "Do not disconnect," "Eject Before Disconnecting," or "Sync in Progress." You can safely disconnect the cable from your iPod if the iPod screen says "OK to disconnect," "Charging," "Charged," or you see the iPod main menu screen.

Synchronize Music

You can synchronize the music in your iTunes Library to your iPod, iPhone, or iPad. If your device has enough free storage space, you can synchronize all your music. However, if free space is limited on your device, you can synchronize just selected playlists to save space. Once the synchronization is complete and you have disconnected your iPod, iPhone, or iPad, you can then play the synced music on the device.

If you purchased music from the iTunes Store using your iPod touch, iPhone, or iPad, iTunes also synchronizes that music to your Mac.

Synchronize Music

1 Click your device in the iTunes Devices list.

2 Click the **Music** tab.

3 Click **Sync Music** (☐ changes to ☑).

4 Click **Selected playlists, artists, albums, and genres** (○ changes to ⊙).

● If you want all your iTunes music on your device, click **Entire music library** (○ changes to ⊙).

5 Click the check box beside each playlist and artist you want to synchronize (☐ changes to ☑).

Note: See the section "Create a Playlist" in Chapter 6 to learn how to add songs to an iTunes playlist.

6 Click the check box beside each album and genre you want to synchronize (☐ changes to ☑).

7 Click **Apply**.

iTunes synchronizes your music to your iPod, iPhone, or iPad.

● The progress of the synchronization appears here.

● When the synchronization is complete, you can disconnect your device.

Is there any way to tell in advance how much storage space the music I am syncing will take up on my device?
Yes. In iTunes, either click the **Music** category or click the playlist you want to sync and then examine the status bar. Besides telling you the number of songs in the library or playlist and their total duration, the status bar displays the total size of the library or playlist (●).

Is there a way to control what music gets synchronized to my iPod Shuffle?
Yes, you can configure iTunes to send a playlist to your iPod Shuffle. Connect your iPod Shuffle, click it in the Devices section, and then click the **Contents** tab. Click the **Autofill From** ⬍, click the playlist you want to send to the device, and then click **Autofill**.

Synchronize Photos to Your Device

You can synchronize the photos on your Mac to your iPod, iPhone, or iPad. If your iPod or iPhone has enough storage capacity, you can synchronize all your photos. If you do not have much free space on your device, you can synchronize just selected albums and events instead. Once the synchronization is complete

and you have disconnected your iPod, iPhone, or iPad, you can view the synced photos on the device.

To learn how to get photos taken with your iPod touch, iPhone, or iPad 2 onto your Mac, see the section "Synchronize Photos from Your Device."

Synchronize Photos to Your Device

① Click your iPod, iPhone, or iPad in the iTunes Devices list.

② Click the **Photos** tab.

③ Click **Sync Photos from** (☐ changes to ☑).

④ Click **Selected albums, events, and faces, and automatically include** (○ changes to ◉).

● If you want all your photos on your device, click **All photos, albums, events, and faces** (○ changes to ◉).

⑤ Click the check box beside each album and event you want to synchronize (☐ changes to ☑).

6 Click the check box beside faces you want to synchronize (☐ changes to ☑).

Note: See the section "Add Names to Faces in Your Photos" in Chapter 8 to learn how to apply faces.

7 Click **Apply**.

iTunes synchronizes your photos to your device.

● The progress of the synchronization appears here.

● When the synchronization is complete, you can disconnect your iPod or iPhone.

Simplify It

How do I sync a folder of photos?
Although it is easiest to sync based on iPhoto albums, events, and faces, you can also synchronize one or more folders.

1 Click the **Sync Photos from** ⁞ and then click **Pictures**.

You can also click **Choose folder**, use the dialog to open the folder, and then click **Choose**.

2 Click **Selected folders** (○ changes to ⊙).

● To synchronize the entire folder, click **All folders** (○ changes to ⊙) instead.

3 Click the check box beside each subfolder you want to synchronize.

☑ Sync Photos from 🖼 Pictures ⁞ — **1**

○ All folders
⊙ Selected folders — **2**
☐ Include videos

Folders

☑ 📁 Bahamas — 166
☐ 📁 Brickworks Pics
☐ 📁 Dickie Lake 2006
☑ 📁 Flat Coat Calendar 2010 — 116
☐ 📁 Flat Coat Calender 2009
☐ 📁 Florence
☑ 📁 Flowers — 8
☐ 📁 Gypsy
☑ 📁 iPhonography — 44
☐ 📁 Photo Booth

3

Synchronize Photos from Your Device

Although you normally want to synchronize photos from your Mac to your iPhone, you can also perform the reverse procedure and sync your iPhone's photos to your Mac.

If you have received photos on your device, or used the built-in camera in a device such as the iPod touch, iPhone, or iPad 2 to take pictures,

you may want to view and work with those pictures on your Mac. To do that, you must use iPhoto to synchronize the photos from your device.

To learn how to synchronize photos from your Mac to your iPod, iPhone, or iPad, see the section "Synchronize Photos to Your Device."

Synchronize Photos from Your Device

1 Connect your device to your Mac.

Note: *See the section "Connect an iPod, iPhone, or iPad," earlier in this chapter.*

Mac OS X automatically launches iPhoto.

● Your device appears in the iPhoto Devices list.

● iPhoto displays your device's Camera Roll photos.

2 Press and hold ⌘ and click each photo you want to import.

3 Use the Event Name text box to type a name for this event.

④ Click **Import Selected**.

● If you want to import every photo from your device, click **Import All** instead.

When the import is complete, iPhoto asks whether you want to keep the original photos on the device.

⑤ Click **Keep Photos**.

● If you are running out of storage space on your device or no longer need the photos on your device, click **Delete Photos** instead.

I keep many photos on my device. Is there a way to make the importing process more manageable?
Yes. If you have imported some of your device photos in the past, you probably do not want to import them again. In that case, you should tell iPhoto to hide those photos that you have previously imported. To do that, click the **Hide photos already imported** check box (☐ changes to ☑).

Is there a way to prevent iPhoto from running every time I connect my device?
Yes. Click **Finder** (🖳), click **Applications** to open the Applications folder, and then double-click **Image Capture**. In the Image Capture application, click the **Connecting this iPhone opens** ⫶ and then click **No application**.

Paul's iPhone	
Connecting this iPhone opens:	
No application	⫶
☐ Delete after import	

Synchronize Movies and TV Shows

If you have a video iPod, an iPhone, or an iPad, you can use iTunes to synchronize movies and TV show episodes to your device. Once the synchronization is complete and you have disconnected your device, you can play the synced movies or TV shows on the device.

Synchronize movies and TV shows with care. A single half-hour TV episode may be as large as 250MB, and full-length movies are several gigabytes, so even a modest video collection will consume lots of storage space on your device.

Synchronize Movies and TV Shows

1 Click your device.

2 Click **Movies**.

3 If you want to view a rented movie on your device, click **Move**.

4 Scroll down and click **Sync Movies** (☐ changes to ☑).

5 Click **Automatically include** (☑ changes to ☐).

6 Click each movie to synchronize (☐ changes to ☑).

7 Click **TV Shows**.

8 Click **Sync TV Shows**
(□ changes to ☑).

9 Click **Automatically
include** (☑ changes to □).

10 Click each TV show to
synchronize (□ changes
to ☑).

11 Click **Apply**.

iTunes synchronizes your
movies and TV shows to
your device.

Simplify It

**Is there a way to synchronize just
the TV shows that I have not
watched yet?**
Click **Automatically include**
(□ changes to ☑), click ↕, and then
click an "unwatched" option (such
as **all unwatched**). An episode is
unwatched if you have not yet viewed
it in iTunes or your device. If you
watch an episode on your device, the
player sends this information to iTunes
when you next sync.

**Why does iTunes not sync some of
my TV show episodes?**
If you selected one of the "unwatched"
options, then iTunes does not sync any
episode marked as watched, which can
occur even if you watch only a few
seconds of an episode. To mark a TV
episode as unwatched, choose the TV
Shows library, right-click the episode,
and then click **Mark as Unwatched**.

Synchronize Contacts, Calendars, and Mail

If you will be away from your Mac, you can stay in touch by synchronizing your contacts, calendars, and e-mail accounts.

The iPod, iPhone, and iPad include both address book features and calendar tools, so you can ensure you are always dealing with the same data by synchronizing your Mac's Address Book contacts and iCal calendars to your iPod, iPhone, or iPad.

The iPod touch, iPhone, and iPad also support e-mail, so you can use the same e-mail on both your Mac and your device by synchronizing one or more e-mail accounts.

Synchronize Contacts, Calendars, and Mail

Synchronize Contacts and Calendars on Your Device

1 Click your device.

2 Click **Info**.

3 Click **Sync Address Book Contacts** (□ changes to ☑).

4 Click **All contacts** (○ changes to ◉).

5 Scroll down and click **Sync iCal Calendars** (□ changes to ☑).

6 Click **All calendars** (○ changes to ◉).

7 Click **Apply**.

iTunes synchronizes your contacts and calendars to your device.

Synchronize E-mail Accounts on Your Device

1 Click your device.

2 Click **Info**.

3 Click **Sync Mail Accounts** (☐ changes to ☑).

4 Click the check box beside each account you want to synchronize (☐ changes to ☑).

5 Click **Apply**.

iTunes synchronizes the selected e-mail accounts to your device.

Is there any other information I can synchronize with my iPhone or iPad?
Yes, you can also synchronize your bookmarks, which are your favorite websites that you have saved using the Safari web browser (see the section "Bookmark Web Pages" in Chapter 3). In iTunes, click your device, click the **Info** tab, scroll down to the Other section, and then click the **Sync Safari bookmarks** check box (☐ changes to ☑).

Synchronize Apps

If you have an iPod touch, iPhone, or iPad, you can download small programs — called *apps*, which is short for *applications* — from Apple's App Store to run on your device. You can do this using the App Store on the device, but you can also download apps using your Mac. In that case, you must synchronize the apps with your device.

Synchronize Apps

① Click your device in the iTunes Devices list.

② Click the **Apps** tab.

③ Click **Sync Apps** (☐ changes to ☑).

4 Click the check box beside each app you want to synchronize (☐ changes to ☑).

5 Click **Apply**.

iTunes synchronizes your apps.

Simplify It

Can I update my apps using my Mac?
Yes. Updating an app means downloading the latest version of the software, which is almost always free. Here are the steps to follow:

1 In iTunes, click **Apps**.

2 Click **X Updates Available**, where *X* is the number of updates.

3 Locate the app you want to update.

4 Click **Get Update**.

● Alternatively, click **Download All Free Updates** to download every available update.

iTunes downloads the update or updates.

Chapter 8

Viewing and Editing Photos

Mac OS X comes with a number of useful tools for working with your photos, including tools that enable you to view your photos, display your photos in a slide show, and take your own picture.

If your Mac comes with the iLife suite, you can also use the iPhoto application to view and edit photos. With iPhoto you can import photos from a digital camera, create an album to display related photos, identify faces in a photo, and send a photo via e-mail. iPhoto also comes with several editing tools that enable you to crop, rotate, and straighten photos, as well as remove red eye from a photo.

View a Preview of a Photo

Mac OS X offers several tools you can use to see a preview of any photo on your Mac.

The Finder application has a number of methods you can use to view your photos, but here you learn about the two easiest methods.

First, you can preview any saved image file using the Mac OS X Quick Look feature; second, you can see photo previews by switching to the Cover Flow view.

You can also preview photos using the Preview application.

View a Preview of a Photo

View a Preview with Quick Look

1 Click **Finder** (⊞) in the Dock.

2 Open the folder that contains the photo you want to preview.

3 Click the photo.

4 Click **Quick Look** (👁).

You can also right-click the photo and then click **Quick Look**, or press Spacebar.

● Finder displays a preview of the photo.

View a Preview with Cover Flow

1 Click **Finder** (⊞) in the Dock.

2 Open the folder that contains the photo you want to preview.

3 Click the photo.

4 Click **Cover Flow** (▥).

● Finder displays a preview of the photo.

● Use the scroll bar to scroll through the other photos in the folder.

View a Preview in the Preview Application

1 Click **Finder** (🖥️) in the Dock.

2 Open the folder that contains the photo you want to preview.

3 Click the photo.

4 Click **File**.

5 Click **Open With**.

6 Click **Preview**.

Note: In many cases, you can also simply double-click the photo to open it in the Preview application.

The Preview application opens and displays the photo.

7 Use the toolbar buttons to change how the photo appears in the Preview window. For example, click **Zoom +** to get a closer look at the photos.

● More commands are available on the View menu.

8 When you are finished viewing the photo, click **Close** (●).

Simplify It

Is there an easier way to preview multiple photos using the Preview application?
Yes, you can load multiple photos into the Preview application. In Finder, navigate to the folder that contains the photos, select each file that you want to preview, and then follow Steps **4** to **6** in this section. In Preview, click **Next** and **Previous** to navigate the photos.

Is there a way that I can zoom in on just a portion of a photo?
Yes. In Preview, click **Tools** and then click **Select Tool** (or either press ⌘ + ③ or click **Select** in the toolbar). Click and drag your mouse (➤) to select the portion of the photo that you want to magnify. Click **View** and then click **Zoom to Selection** (or press ⌘ + ✳).

View a Slide Show of Your Photos

Instead of viewing your photos one at a time, you can easily view multiple photos by running them in a slide show.

You can run the slide show using the Preview application. The slide show displays each photo for a few seconds, and then Preview automatically displays the next photo. Quick Look also offers several on-screen controls that you can use to control the slide show playback. You can also configure Quick Look to display the images full-screen.

View a Slide Show of Your Photos

① Click **Finder** (🖼) in the Dock.

② Open the folder that contains the photos you want to view in the slide show.

③ Select the photos you want to view.

④ Click **File**.

⑤ Click **Open With**.

⑥ Click **Preview**.

The Preview window appears.

⑦ Click **View**.

⑧ Click **Slideshow**.

You can also select Slideshow by pressing Shift + ⌘ + F.

Preview opens the slide show window.

9 Move the mouse (🡡).

● Preview displays the slide show controls.

10 Click **Play**.

Preview begins the slide show.

● Click **Next** to move to the next photo.

● Click **Back** to move to the previous photo.

● Click **Pause** to suspend the slide show.

11 When the slide show is over or when you want to return to Finder, click **Close** or press Esc.

Simplify It

Can I jump to a specific photo during the slide show?
Yes. With the slide show running, press Return to stop the show and display thumbnail views of all the slide show images. Use the arrow keys to select the photo that you want to view in the slide show, and then press Return. Preview returns you to the slide show and displays the selected photo. Click **Play** to resume the slide show from that photo.

What keyboard shortcuts can I use when viewing a slide show?
Press ➡ to display the next photo, and press ⬅ to display the previous photo. Press Spacebar to pause the slide show, and press Spacebar to resume. Press Esc to end the slide show.

Open and Close iPhoto

If your Mac has iLife installed, the suite includes the iPhoto application, which offers special tools for viewing, managing, and editing your photos. You can also purchase iPhoto separately through the App Store. With iPhoto you can import photos from a digital camera, view and organize the photos on your Mac, and edit and repair photos.

To begin using the program, you must first learn how to find and open the iPhoto window. When you finish using the program, you can close the iPhoto window to free up computer processing power.

Open and Close iPhoto

Open iPhoto

1 In the Dock, click **iPhoto** (▣).

The iPhoto window appears.

The first time you launch iPhoto, the program asks if you want to use iPhoto when you connect your digital camera.

2 Click **Yes**.

The first time you launch iPhoto, the program asks if you want to view your photos on a map.

3 If you have a GPS-enabled camera (such as an iPhone 4, 3GS, or 3G, or an iPad 2 with 3G) or if you want to enter location data by hand, click **Yes**.

Close iPhoto

1 Click **iPhoto**.

2 Click **Quit iPhoto**.

Are there other methods I can use to open iPhoto?
If you do not have ![icon] in the Dock, there are a couple of methods you can use to open iPhoto. If you have used iPhoto recently, to click ![apple], click **Recent Items**, and then click **iPhoto**. Alternatively, click **Spotlight** (![q]), type **iphoto**, and then click **iPhoto** in the search results.

Are there faster methods I can use to close iPhoto?
Probably the fastest method you can use to quit iPhoto is to click ![o]. Alternatively, right-click the **iPhoto** icon (![icon]) and then click **Quit**. Finally, if your hands are closer to the keyboard than to the mouse, you can quit iPhoto by switching to the applications and pressing ![⌘] + ![Q].

Import Photos from a Digital Camera

You can import photos from a digital camera and save them on your Mac. If you have the iLife suite installed on your Mac, you can use the iPhoto application to handle importing photos. iPhoto is also available separately through the App Store. iPhoto enables you to add a name and a description to each import, which helps you to find your photos after the import is complete.

To perform the import, you will need a cable to connect your digital camera to your Mac. Most digital cameras come with a USB cable.

Import Photos from a Digital Camera

Import Photos from the Digital Camera

1 Connect one end of the cable to the digital camera.

2 Connect the other end of the cable to a free USB port on your Mac.

3 Turn the camera on and put it in either playback or computer mode.

Your Mac launches the iPhoto application.

● Your digital camera appears in the Devices section.

● iPhoto displays previews of the camera's photos.

4 Use the Event Name text box to type a name for the group of photos you are going to import.

5 Select the photos that you want to import.

Note: To select photos, either click and drag the mouse ( ) around the photos you want, or press and hold ⌘ and click each photo.

6 Click **Import Selected**.

● To import all the camera's photos, click **Import All** instead.

iPhoto imports the photos from the camera.

iPhoto asks if you want to delete the original photos from the camera.

7 If you no longer need the photos on the camera, click **Delete Photos**.

● If you prefer to keep the photos on the camera, click **Keep Photos** instead.

View the Imported Photos

1 Click **Events**.

2 Double-click the event name that you specified in Step **4**.

Simplify It

When I connect my digital camera, why do I see Image Capture instead of iPhoto?
You need to configure Image Capture to open iPhoto when you connect your camera. Follow these steps:

1 Connect your digital camera to your Mac.

The Image Capture application opens.

*Note: If you do not see the Image Capture application, click **Finder** ( ) in the Dock, click **Applications**, and then double-click **Image Capture**.*

2 Click the **Connecting** and then click **iPhoto**.

3 Click **Image Capture** in the menu bar.

4 Click **Quit Image Capture**.

View Your Photos

If you want to look at several photos, you can use the iPhoto application, which is available with Apple's iLife suite or separately via the App Store.

iPhoto offers a feature called full-screen mode, which hides everything else and displays your photos using the entire screen. Once you

activate full-screen mode, iPhoto offers several on-screen controls that you can use to navigate backward and forward through the photos in a folder. iPhoto's full-screen mode also shows thumbnail images of each photo, so you can quickly jump to any photo you want to view.

View Your Photos

1 In iPhoto, click **Events**.

2 Double-click the event that contains the photos you want to view.

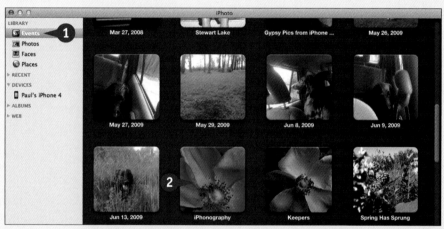

3 Double-click the first photo you want to view.

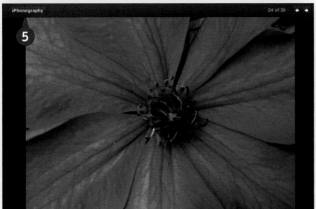

iPhoto displays the photo.

④ Click **Next** (▶) to view the next photo in the event.

● You can also click **Previous** (◀) to see the previous photo in the Event.

Note: *You can also navigate photos by pressing ▶ and ◀.*

⑤ When you are done, click the name of the event.

Simplify It

Is there a way that I can jump quickly to a particular photo in full-screen mode?
Yes. Follow these steps:

① Move the mouse (▸) to the top of the screen.

● iPhoto displays thumbnail images of the Event's photos.

② Use the horizontal scroll bar to bring the thumbnail of the photo you want into view.

③ Click the photo's thumbnail.

iPhoto displays the photo in full-screen mode.

Create an Album

You can use the iPhoto application to organize your photos into albums. You can get iPhoto either via the iLife suite, which is installed on all new Macs, or via the App Store.

In iPhoto, an *album* is a collection of photos that are usually related in some way. For example, you might create an album for a series of vacation photos, for photos taken at a party or other special event, or for photos that include a particular person, pet, or place.

Using your iPhoto Library, you can create customized albums that include only the photos that you want to view.

Create an Album

Create the Album

1 Click **File**.

2 Click **New**.

3 Click **Album**.

Note: You can also start a new album by pressing ⌘ + N*.*

4 Type a name for the new album.

5 Press Return.

Add Photos to the Album

1 Click **Photos**.

2 Click ► beside an event that contains photos you want to work with (► changes to ▼).

3 Click and drag a photo and drop it on the new album.

4 Repeat Steps **2** and **3** to add other photos to the album.

5 Click the album.

● iPhoto displays the photos you added to the album.

Simplify It

Is there any way to make iPhoto add photos to an album automatically?
Yes, you can create a *smart album* where the photos that appear in the album have one or more properties in common, such as the description, rating, date, or text in the photo title. Click **File**, click **New**, and then click **Smart Album** (you can also press Option + ⌘ + N). Use the Smart Album dialog to create one or more rules that define which photos you want to appear in the album.

Crop a Photo

If you have a photo containing elements that you do not want or need to see, you can often cut out those elements. This is called *cropping*, and you can do this with iPhoto, which comes with the iLife suite or via the App Store.

When you crop a photo, you specify a rectangular area of the photo that you want to keep. iPhoto discards everything outside of the rectangle.

Cropping is a useful skill to have because it can help give focus to the true subject of a photo. Cropping is also useful for removing extraneous elements that appear on or near the edges of a photo.

Crop a Photo

1 Click the photo you want to crop.

2 Click **Edit** (✏️).

iPhoto displays its editing tools.

3 Click **Crop** (▣).

iPhoto displays a cropping rectangle on the photo.

④ Click and drag a corner or side to define the area you want to keep.

Note: *Remember that iPhoto keeps the area inside the rectangle.*

⑤ Click **Done**.

iPhoto saves the cropped photo.

⑥ Click ✎.

iPhoto exits edit mode.

Simplify It

Is there a quick way to crop a photo to a certain size?
Yes, iPhoto enables you to specify either a specific size, such as 640 x 480, or a specific ratio, such as 4 x 3 or 16 x 9. Follow these steps:

① Follow Steps **1** to **3** to display the Crop tool.

② Click the **Constrain** check box (☐ changes to ☑).

③ In the Constrain list, click ↕.

④ Click the size or ratio you want to use.

⑤ Click **Done**.

⑥ Click ✎.

iPhoto exits edit mode.

Rotate a Photo

You can rotate a photo using the iPhoto application, which comes with all new Macs as part of iLife, and is also available separately via the App Store.

Depending on how you held your camera when you took a shot, the resulting photo might show the subject sideways or upside down. This may be the effect you want, but more likely this is a problem. To fix this problem, you can use iPhoto to rotate the photo so that the subject appears right-side up. You can rotate a photo either clockwise or counterclockwise.

Rotate a Photo

① Click the photo you want to rotate.

② Click **Edit** (✎).

iPhoto displays its editing tools.

3 Click **Rotate** (🔄).

iPhoto rotates the photo 90 degrees counterclockwise.

4 Repeat Step **3** until the subject of the photo is right-side up.

5 Click 🖊.

iPhoto exits edit mode.

Simplify It

Can I rotate a photo clockwise instead?
Yes, you can:

1 With the editing tools displayed, press and hold the `Option` key.

The Rotate icon changes from 🔄 to 🔁.

2 With `Option` held down, click **Rotate** to rotate the photo clockwise by 90 degrees.

Note: *You can also right-click the photo and then click **Rotate Clockwise**.*

Straighten a Photo

You can straighten a crooked photo using the iPhoto application, which comes with all new Macs as part of iLife, and is also available separately via the App Store.

If you do not use a tripod when taking pictures, getting your camera perfectly level when you take a shot is very difficult and requires lots of

practice and a steady hand. Despite your best efforts, you might end up with a photo that is not quite level. To fix this problem, you can use iPhoto to nudge the photo clockwise or counterclockwise so that the subject appears straight.

Straighten a Photo

1 Click the photo you want to straighten.

2 Click **Edit** (✐).

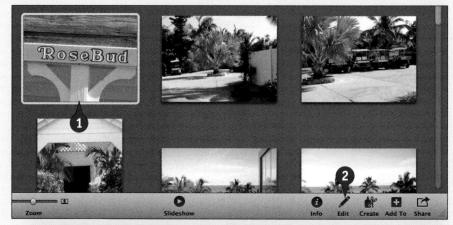

iPhoto displays its editing tools.

3 Click **Straighten** (▣).

iPhoto displays a grid over the photo.

④ Click and drag the **Angle** slider.

Drag the slider to the left to angle the photo counterclockwise.

Drag the slider to the right to angle the photo clockwise.

⑤ Click **Done**.

⑥ Click ✎.

iPhoto exits edit mode.

How do I know when my photo is level?
Use the gridlines that iPhoto places over the photo. Locate a horizontal line in your photo, and then rotate the photo so that this line is parallel to the nearest horizontal line in the grid. You can also match a vertical line in the photo with a vertical line in the grid.

Remove Red Eye from a Photo

You can remove red eye from a photo using the iPhoto application, which comes with all new Macs as part of iLife, and is also available separately via the App Store.

When you use a flash to take a picture of one or more people, in some cases the flash may reflect off the subjects' retinas. The result is the common phenomenon of *red eye*, where each person's pupils appear as red instead of black.

If you have a photo where one or more people have red eyes due to the camera flash, you can use iPhoto to remove the red eye and give your subjects a more natural look.

Remove Red Eye from a Photo

1. Click the photo that contains the red eye.

2. Click **Edit** (✎).

iPhoto displays its editing tools.

○ If needed, you can click and drag this slider to the right to zoom in on the picture.

● You can click and drag this rectangle to bring the red eye into view.

3. Click **Fix Red-Eye** (▣).

iPhoto displays its Red-Eye controls.

● You may be able to fix the red eye automatically by clicking the **Auto-fix red-eye** check box. If that does not work, continue with the rest of these steps.

④ Move the red eye pointer over a red eye in the photo.

⑤ Click the red eye.

● iPhoto removes the red eye.

⑥ Repeat Steps **4** and **5** to fix any other instances of red eye in the photo.

⑦ Click **Done**.

⑧ Click 🖉.

iPhoto exits edit mode.

Simplify It

Why does iPhoto remove only part of the red eye in my photo when I click it with the Red-Eye tool?
The Red-Eye tool may not be set to a large enough size. The tool should be approximately the same size as the subject's eye:

① Follow Steps **1** to **3** to display the Red-Eye controls.

② Click and drag the Size slider until the Red-Eye tool is the size of the red-eye area.

③ Use your mouse to move the circle over the red eye and then click.

iPhoto removes the red eye that occurs within the circle.

Add Names to Faces in Your Photos

You can make your photos easier to manage and navigate by adding names to the faces that appear in each photo. This is sometimes called *tagging*, and it enables you to navigate your photos by name. For example, you can view all your photos in which a certain person appears.

To add names to the faces in your photos, you must be using iPhoto '09 or later. To check this, click iPhoto in the menu bar and then click About iPhoto.

Add Names to Faces in Your Photos

① Click the photo that you want to tag.

② Click **Info** (ⓘ).

③ Click **X unnamed** (where X is the number of faces iPhoto identifies in the photo).

iPhoto displays its naming tools.

④ Click **unnamed**.

5 Type the person's name.

6 Press `Return`.

7 Repeat Steps **3** to **5** to name each person in the photo.

● If iPhoto did not mark a face in the photo, click **Add a Face**, size and position the box over the face, then type the name in the **click to name** box.

8 Click **Info**.

iPhoto exits naming mode.

Simplify It

How do I view all the photos that contain a particular person?
One method you can use is to open a photo, click **Info** (●), and then click the **Show All** arrow (●) that appears beside the person's name. You can also follow these steps:

1 Click **Faces** in the iPhoto Sidebar.

● iPhoto displays the names and sample photos of each person you have named.

2 Double-click the person you want to view.

iPhoto displays all the photos that contain the person.

E-mail a Photo

You can use the iPhoto application to create a message to send a photo to another person via e-mail. iPhoto comes with all new Macs as part of iLife, and is also available separately via the App Store.

If you have a photo that you want to share with someone, and you know that person's e-mail address, you can send the photo in an e-mail message. Using iPhoto, you can specify which photo you want to send, and iPhoto will create a new message.

Even if a photo is very large, you can still send it via e-mail because you can use iPhoto to shrink the copy of the photo that appears in the message.

E-mail a Photo

1 Click the photo you want to send.

2 Click **Share**.

3 Click **Email**.

● You can also click **Share** (⬆) and then click **Email**.

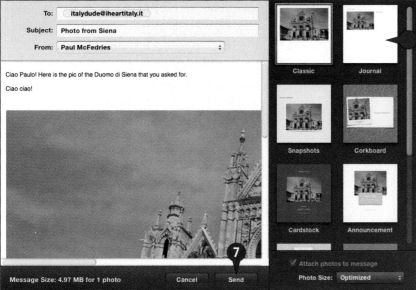

● iPhoto creates a new message.

● The photo appears in the message body.

❹ Use the To text box to type the address of the message recipient.

❺ Use the Subject text box to type the message subject.

❻ Click here and then type your message text.

● You can use these controls to format the text.

● You can click these thumbnails to apply a special effect to the message.

❼ Click **Send**.

iPhoto sends the message.

How do I change the size of the photo?
You need to be careful when sending photos because a single image can be several megabytes in size. If your recipient's e-mail system places restrictions on the size of messages it can receive, your message might not go through.

To change the size of the photo, click the **Photo Size** ⬦ and then click the size you want to use for the sent photo, such as Small or Medium. Note that this does not affect the size of the original photo, just the copy that is sent with the message.

Take Your Picture

You can use your Mac to take a picture of yourself. If your Mac comes with a built-in iSight camera, or if you have an external camera attached to your Mac, you can use the camera to take a picture of yourself using the Photo Booth application.

Once you have taken your picture, you can e-mail that picture, add it to iPhoto, or set is as your user account or iChat buddy picture.

Take Your Picture

Take Your Picture with Photo Booth

1 In the Dock, click **Photo Booth** (📷).

The Photo Booth window appears.

● The live feed from the camera appears here.

2 Click **Take a still picture** (▫).

● Click **Take four quick pictures** (▦) if you want Photo Booth to snap four successive photos, each about 1 second apart.

● Click **Take a movie clip** (▣) if you want Photo Booth to capture the live camera feed as a movie.

3 Click **Take Photo** (⬤).

Photo Booth counts down
3 seconds and then takes the photo.

Note: *When the Mac is taking your
picture, be sure to look into the
camera, not into the screen.*

Work with Your Photo Booth Picture

● Photo Booth displays the picture.

1 Click the taken picture.

● Click **Email** (▣) to send the photo in
an e-mail message.

● Click **iPhoto** (▣) to add the photo to
iPhoto.

● Click **Account Picture** (👥) to set the
photo as your user account picture.

● Click **Buddy Picture** (▣) to set the
photo as your iChat buddy picture.

Can I make my photos more interesting?
Definitely. Photo Booth comes with around two dozen
special effects that can make your photo look like an
X-ray or comic book, apply distortions such as a mirror
image, add a background image, and more. Follow
these steps:

1 In Photo Booth, click **Effects**.

2 Click an icon to select a different page of
effects.

● You can also use the arrow buttons to change
pages.

3 Click the effect you want to use.

Chapter 9

Playing and Creating Digital Video

Mac OS X comes with the tools you need to play movies and digital video, including the DVD Player and QuickTime Player applications.

If you have Apple's iLife suite installed on your Mac, you can also create your own digital video movies. Using the iMovie application that comes with the iLife suite, you can import camcorder video to your Mac and use that video as the raw footage for your movie. With iMovie you can then apply scene transitions and add titles, credits, and a soundtrack.

Play a DVD Using DVD Player

If your Mac has a DVD drive, you can insert a DVD movie disc into the drive and then use the DVD Player application to play the movie on your Mac.

You can either watch the movie in full-screen mode where the movie takes up the entire Mac screen, or you can play the DVD in a window while you work on other things. DVD Player has features that enable you to control the movie playback and volume.

Play a DVD Using DVD Player

Play a DVD Full-Screen

1 Insert the DVD disc into your Mac's DVD drive.

DVD Player runs automatically and starts playing the DVD full-screen.

2 If you get to the DVD menu, click **Play** to start the movie.

3 Move the ▸ to the bottom of the screen.

The playback controls appear.

● Click to pause the movie.

● Click to fast-forward the movie.

● Click to rewind the movie.

● Drag the slider to adjust the volume.

● Click to display the DVD menu.

● Click to exit full-screen mode.

Play a DVD in a Window

① Insert the DVD disc into your Mac's DVD drive.

DVD Player runs automatically and starts playing the DVD full-screen.

② Press ⌘ + F.

DVD Player displays the movie in a window.

● DVD Player displays the Controller.

③ When you get to the DVD menu, click **Play Movie** to start the movie.

● Click to pause the movie.

● Click and hold to fast-forward the movie.

● Click and hold to rewind the movie.

● Drag the slider to adjust the volume.

● Click to display the DVD menu.

● Click to stop the movie.

● Click to eject the DVD.

How can I always start my DVDs in a window?

① Press ⌘ + F to switch to the window view.

② Click **DVD Player** in the menu bar.

③ Click **Preferences** to open the DVD Player preferences.

④ Click the **Player** tab.

⑤ Click **Enter Full Screen mode** (☑ changes to ☐).

⑥ If you want to control when the playback starts, also click **Start playing disc** (☑ changes to ☐).

⑦ Click **OK** to put the new settings into effect.

Play Digital Video with QuickTime Player

Your Mac comes with an application called QuickTime Player that can play digital video files in various formats. You will mostly use QuickTime Player to play digital video files stored on your Mac, but you can also use the application to play digital video from the web.

QuickTime Player enables you to open video files, navigate the digital video playback, and control the digital video volume.

Although you learn only how to play digital video files in this task, the version of QuickTime that comes with Mac OS X 10.7 (Lion) comes with many extra features, including the capability to record movies and audio and to cut and paste scenes.

Play Digital Video with QuickTime Player

① Click **Finder** (🗔).

② Click **Applications**.

③ Double-click **QuickTime Player**.

The QuickTime Player application appears.

④ Click **File**.

⑤ Click **Open File**.

You can also press ⌘ + O.

The Open dialog appears.

⑥ Locate and click the video file you want to play.

⑦ Click **Open**.

QuickTime opens a new player window.

⑧ Click **Play** (▶).

● Click here to fast-forward the video.

● Click here to rewind the video.

● Click and drag this slider to adjust the volume.

If you want to view the video in full-screen mode, press ⌘ + Ⓕ.

Can I use QuickTime Player to play a video from the web?
Yes, as long as you know the Internet address of the video, QuickTime Player can play most video formats available on the web. In QuickTime Player, click **File** and then click **Open Location** (or press ⌘ + Ⓤ). In the Open URL dialog, type or paste the video address in the Movie Location text box, and then click **Open**.

Create a New Movie Project

If you have the iLife suite installed on your Mac, the suite includes iMovie, which enables you to import video from a digital camcorder or video file and use that footage to create your own movies. You do this by first creating a project that holds your video clips, transitions, titles, and other elements of your movie.

When you first start iMovie, the program creates a new project for you automatically. Follow the steps in this section to create subsequent projects.

Create a New Movie Project

① Click the **iMovie** icon (◼) in the Dock.

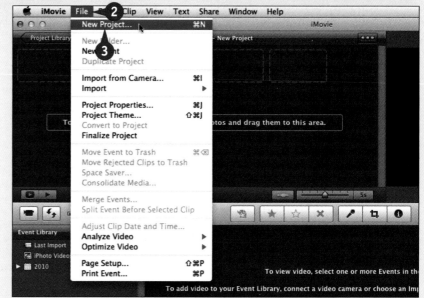

The iMovie window appears.

② Click **File**.

③ Click **New Project**.

You can also press ⌘ + N.

The New Project dialog appears.

4 Use the Name text box to type a name for your project.

5 Click the **Aspect Ratio** ⬩ and then click the ratio you prefer: Widescreen (16:9) or Standard (4:3).

6 If you want to apply a theme to your project, click the one you want in the Project Themes list.

7 If you want iMovie to automatically insert transitions between all your clips, click **Automatically add** (☐ changes to ☑) and then click ⬩ to choose the type of transition.

If you chose a theme in Step **6**, the name of the check box changes to Automatically add transition and titles, and iMovie selects it by default.

8 Click **Create**.

iMovie creates your new project.

What are the iMovie themes?
Each theme comes with its own set of titles and transitions that get added automatically, saving you lots of work. There are seven themes in all, including Photo Album, Bulletin Board, Comic Book, and Scrapbook. If one of them is suitable for your project, applying it cuts down on your production time.

How do I switch from one project to another?
You use the Project Library, which is a list of your movie projects. To display it, click **Window** and then click **Show Project Library**. You can also click the **Project Library** button in the top left corner of the iMovie window. In the Project Library, double-click the project you want to work with.

Import a Video File

With the iMovie application, you can import digital video from a camera for use in your movie project.

If you have video content on a USB digital camcorder or smartphone (such as an iPhone 3GS or later), you can connect the device to your Mac and then import some or all of the video to your iMovie project.

If your Mac has a built-in iSight camera, you can also use iMovie to import live images from that camera to use as digital video footage in your movie project.

Import a Video File

Import all Clips

1 Connect the video device to your Mac.

iMovie displays its Import From dialog.

2 Click **Import All**.

iMovie prompts you to create a new event.

3 Click **Create new Event** (○ changes to ◉).

4 Use the Create new Event text box to type a name for the import event.

● If you want to add the video to an existing event, click **Add to existing Event** (○ changes to ◉) and then choose the event from the pop-up menu.

5 Click **Import**.

Import Selected Clips

1. Connect the video device to your Mac.

   iMovie displays its Import From dialog.

2. Click **Manual**.

3. Deselect the check box under each clip you do not want to import (☑ changes to ☐).

4. Click **Import Checked**.

   iMovie prompts you to create a new event.

5. Click **Create new Event** (○ changes to ◉).

6. Use the Create new Event text box to type a name for the import event.

7. Click **Import**.

   iMovie begins importing the clips.

8. Click **OK**.

9. Click **Done**.

Simplify It

How do I import digital video from my iSight camera?

1. In iMovie, click **File** and then click **Import from Camera**.

2. Click **Capture**.

3. Follow Steps **5** and **6** on this page.

4. Click **Capture**.

5. When you are done, click **Stop**.

6. Click **Done**.

Add Video Clips to Your Project

To create and work with a movie project in iMovie, you must first add some video clips to that project.

A *video clip* is a segment of digital video. You begin building your movie by adding one or more video clips to your project.

When you import digital video as described in the previous section, iMovie automatically breaks up the video into separate clips, with each clip being the footage shot during a single recording session. You can then decide which of those clips you want to add to your project, or you can add only part of a clip.

Add Video Clips to Your Project

Add an Entire Clip

1 Click the Event Library item that contains the video clip you want to add.

2 Press and hold Option and click the clip.

● iMovie selects the entire clip.

3 Click and drag the selected clip and drop it in your project at the spot where you want the clip to appear.

● iMovie adds the entire video clip to the project.

● iMovie adds an orange bar to the bottom of the original clip to indicate that it has been added to the project.

Add a Partial Clip

1 Click the Event Library item that contains the video clip you want to add.

2 Click the clip at the point where you want the selection to begin.

3 Click and drag the right edge of the selection box to the point where you want the selection to end.

4 Click and drag the selected clip and drop it in your project at the spot where you want the clip to appear.

● iMovie adds the selected portion of the video clip to the project.

● iMovie adds an orange bar to the bottom of the original clip to indicate that it has been added to a project.

Is it possible to play a clip before I add it?
Yes. Click the clip at the point where you want the playback to start and then press Spacebar. Press Spacebar again to stop the playback. To see only a portion of the clip, follow Steps **2** and **3** on this page to make your selection, right-click the clip, and then click **Play Selection**.

I added a clip in the wrong place. Can I move it?
Yes. Click the added clip to select it. Use your mouse ( ) to click and drag the clip and then drop the clip in the correct location within the project. To delete the clip from the project, click it, click **Edit**, and then click **Delete Entire Clip** (or press Option + Del).

Trim
a Clip

If you have a video clip that is too long or contains footage you do not need, you can shorten the clip or remove the extra footage. Removing parts of a video clip is called *trimming* the clip.

Trimming a clip is particularly useful if you recorded extra, unneeded footage before and after the action you were trying to capture. By trimming this unneeded footage, your movie will include only the scenes you really require.

Trim a Clip

1. In your project, click the clip you want to trim.

● iMovie selects the entire clip.

2. Use your mouse ( ) to click and drag the left edge of the selection box to the starting position of the part of the clip you want to keep.

3. Use your mouse ( ) to click and drag the right edge of the selection box to the ending position of the part of the clip you want to keep.

④ Click **Clip**.

⑤ Click **Trim to Selection**.

Note: *You can also press* ⌘ + B.

● iMovie trims the clip.

Simplify It

Is it possible to trim a certain number of frames from a clip?
Yes, iMovie enables you to trim one frame at a time from either the beginning or the end of the clip. Follow these steps:

① In your project, click the clip you want to trim.

iMovie selects the entire clip.

② Click **Clip**.

③ Click **Trim Clip End**.

④ Select the trim direction:

● To trim from the beginning, click **Move Left** (or press Option + ◀).

● To trim from the end, click **Move Right** (or press Option + ▶).

iMovie trims the clip.

⑤ Repeat Step **4** until you reach the number of frames that you want to trim.

Add a Transition Between Clips

You can use the iMovie application to enhance the visual appeal of your digital movie by inserting transitions between some or all of the project's video clips.

By default, iMovie jumps immediately from the end of one clip to the beginning of the next clip, a transition called a *jump cut*. You can add more visual interest to your movie by adding a transition between the two clips.

iMovie offers 24 different transitions, including various fades, wipes, and dissolves. More transitions are available if you applied a theme to your iMovie project.

Add a Transition Between Clips

1 Click the **Transitions Browser** button (⌐), or press ⌘ + 4.

● iMovie displays the available transitions.

Note: *To see a preview of a transition, position your mouse (⬉) over the transition thumbnail.*

2 Use your mouse (⬉) to click and drag a transition and drop it between the two clips.

● iMovie adds an icon for the transition between the two clips.

③ Position your mouse (▸) over the beginning of the transition and move the ▸ to the right.

● iMovie displays a preview of the transition.

Simplify It

Can I change the duration of the transition?
Yes. The default length is half a second, but you can increase or decrease the duration by following these steps:

① Double-click the transition icon in your project.

The Inspector appears.

② Use the Duration text box to set the number of seconds you want the transition to take.

③ If you want to change only the current transition, click **Applies to all transitions** (☑ changes to ☐).

④ Click **Done**.

Add a Photo

You can use the iMovie application to enhance your movie projects with still photos.

Although most movie projects consist of several video clips, you can also add a photo to your project. By default, iMovie displays the photo for 4 seconds.

You can also specify how the photo fits in the movie frame: You can adjust the size of the photo to fit the frame, you can crop the photo, or you can apply a Ken Burns effect — which automatically pans and zooms the photo — to animate the static photo.

Add a Photo

1 Click the **Photos Browser** button (⌂), or press ⌘ + ②.

● iMovie displays the available photos.

2 Click the event or album that contains the photo you want to add.

3 Click and drag the photo and drop it inside your project.

● iMovie adds the photo to the movie.

4 Click the photo.

5 Click the **Crop** button (⌂).

iMovie displays the cropping options for the photo.

6 Click **Ken Burns**.

● You can also click **Fit** to have iMovie adjust the size of the photo to fit the movie frame.

● You can also click **Crop** and then click and drag the cropping rectangle to specify how much of the photo you want to appear in the movie frame.

7 Click and drag the green rectangle to set the start point of the Ken Burns animation.

8 Click and drag the red rectangle to set the end point of the Ken Burns animation.

Note: Click and drag the corners and edges of the rectangle to change the size; click and drag the interior of the rectangles to change the position.

● The arrow shows the direction of motion.

9 Click **Done**.

Simplify It

Can I change the length of time that the photo appears in the movie?
Yes. The default length is 4 seconds, but you can increase or decrease the duration by following these steps:

1 Double-click the photo in your project.

2 Click **Clip**.

3 Use the Duration text box to set the number of seconds you want the photo to appear.

4 To change the duration for all the photos in your project, click **Applies to all stills** (□ changes to ☑).

5 Click **Done**.

Add a Music Track

Using the iMovie application, you can enhance the audio component of your movie by adding one or more songs that play in the background. With iMovie you can also add sound effects and other audio files that you feel would enhance your project's audio track.

To get the best audio experience, you can adjust various sound properties. For example, you can adjust the volume of the music clip or the volume of the video clip. You can also use iMovie to adjust the time it takes for the song clip to fade in and fade out.

Add a Music Track

1 Click the **Music and Sound Effect Browser** button (♫), or press ⌘ + 1 .

● iMovie displays the available audio files.

2 Click the folder, category, or playlist that contains the track you want to add.

3 Use your mouse (▸) to click and drag the song and drop it on a video clip.

● iMovie adds the song to the movie.

Note: *iMovie treats the song like a clip, which means you can trim the song as needed, as described earlier in the "Trim a Clip" section.*

4 Double-click the music clip.

iMovie displays the Inspector.

5 Click the **Audio** tab.

6 Use the Volume slider to adjust the volume of the music clip.

7 If you want to reduce the video clip volume, click **Ducking** (□ changes to ☑) and then click and drag the slider.

8 To adjust the fade-in time, click **Fade In: Manual** (□ changes to ☑) and then click and drag the slider.

9 To adjust the fade-out time, click **Fade Out: Manual** (□ changes to ☑) and then click and drag the slider.

10 Click **Done**.

Simplify It

When I add a video clip before the music clip, the music does not play with the new video clip. How can I work around this?

You need to add your song as a background track instead of a clip. Follow these steps:

1 Click ♫.

2 Use your mouse (k) to click and drag a song.

3 Drop the song on the project background, not on a clip or between two clips.

● The background turns green when you have the song positioned correctly.

Record a Voiceover

You can use the iMovie application to augment the audio portion of your movie with a voiceover. A *voiceover* is a voice recording that you make using audio equipment attached to your Mac.

A voiceover is useful for explaining a video clip, introducing the movie, or giving the viewer background information about the movie.

To record a voiceover, your Mac must either have a built-in microphone, such as the one that comes with the iSight camera, or an external microphone connected via an audio jack, USB port, or Bluetooth.

Record a Voiceover

1 If your Mac does not have a built-in microphone, attach a microphone.

Note: *You may need to configure the microphone as the sound input device. Click* **System Preferences** *(), click* **Sound**, *click* **Input**, *and then click your microphone.*

2 Click the **Voiceover** button ().

The Voiceover dialog appears.

3 Click the spot in the movie at which you want the voiceover to begin.

iMovie counts down and then begins the recording.

④ Speak your voiceover text into the microphone.

The progress of the recording appears here.

⑤ When you are finished, click **Recording**.

iMovie adds the voiceover to the clip.

⑥ Click **Close** (⊗).

You can double-click the voiceover to adjust the audio, as described in the previous section.

Simplify It

Is there a way to tell if my voice is too loud or too soft?
Yes, you can use the controls in the Voiceover dialog. You check your voice level by talking into the microphone and then watching the Left and Right volume meters:

● If you see no green bars or just a few green bars, your voice level is too low.

● If you see yellow or red bars, your voice level is too high.

Use the Input Volume slider to adjust the voice level up or down, as needed.

Add Titles and Credits

You can use the iMovie application to enhance your movie project with titles and scrolling credits.

You can get your movie off to a proper start by adding a title and a subtitle at or near the beginning of the movie. iMovie offers a number of title styles that you can choose from, and you can also change the title font.

You can also enhance your movie with *scrolling credits*. This is a special type of title that you place at the end of the movie and that scrolls the names of the people responsible for the project.

Add Titles and Credits

1 Click the **Titles browser** button (T).

● iMovie displays the available title types.

2 Use your mouse (▶) to click and drag a title and drop it where you want the titles to appear.

Note: *To see just the titles, drop the title thumbnail at the beginning of the movie or between two clips. To superimpose the titles on a video clip, drop the title thumbnail on the clip.*

● If you want to add credits, click and drag the **Scrolling Credits** thumbnail and drop it at the end of the movie.

● iMovie adds a clip for the title.

3 Replace this text with the movie title.

4 Replace this text with the movie subtitle.

5 Click **Done**.

Note: iMovie treats the title like a clip, which means you can lengthen or shorten the title duration by clicking and dragging the beginning or end, as described earlier in the "Trim a Clip" section.

How do I change the font of the titles?
The Text menu offers several font-related commands, including Bold, Italic, Bigger, and Smaller. You can also click the **Show Fonts** command to display the Fonts dialog. If you do not see the Fonts dialog shown here, you can switch to iMovie's predefined fonts by clicking **iMovie Font Panel**. You can then click a typeface, font color, and type size; click **Done** (●) to close the dialog.

Choose Font		
Helvetica Neue		1
Futura Medium		2
Impact		3
Coolvetica		4
Sign Painter House Script		5
Chalkboard		6
American Typewriter		7
Big Caslon Medium		8
Baskerville		9

Play the Movie

The iMovie application offers the Viewer pane, which you can use to play your movie.

While you are building your iMovie project, it is a good idea to occasionally play some or all of the movie to check your progress. For example, you can play the entire movie to make sure the video and audio are working properly and are synchronized correctly. You can also play parts of the movie to ensure that your transitions appear when you want them to.

Play the Movie

Play from the Beginning

1. Click **View**.

2. Click **Play from Beginning**.

    Note: You can also press ⟨\⟩ or click the **Play Project from beginning** button (▶).

Play from a Specific Location

1. Position the mouse ⟨k⟩ over the spot where you want to start playing the movie.

2. Press ⟨Spacebar⟩.

Play a Selection

1 Select the video clips you want to play.

Note: See the first tip below to learn how to select multiple video clips.

2 Click **View**.

3 Click **Play Selection**.

Note: You can also press [/].

How do I select multiple video clips?

Press and hold [⌘] and then click anywhere inside each clip you want to select. If you select a clip by accident, [⌘] + click it again to deselect it. To skip just a few clips, first press [⌘] + [A] to select all the clips, then press and hold [⌘] and click the clips you do not want in the selection.

How do I add my movie to a DVD disc?

First, insert a blank DVD in your Mac's DVD drive. If your Mac asks what action you want to take with the blank DVD, click **Ignore**. In iMovie, click **Share** and then click **iDVD**. iMovie creates your movie and then sends it to iDVD.

Chapter 10

Customizing Mac OS X to Suit Your Style

Although your Mac works well right out of the box, there may be some aspects of the system that do not suit you. For example, you might not like the default desktop background or the layout of the Dock. For these and other changes, Mac OS X comes with a number of features that enable you to customize your Mac. Not only can you change the appearance of Mac OS X to suit your taste, but you can also change the way Mac OS X works to make it easier and more efficient for you to use.

Display System Preferences

You can find many of the Mac OS X customization features in System Preferences, a collection of settings and options that control the overall look and operation of Mac OS X.

You can use System Preferences to change the desktop background, specify a screen saver, set your Mac's sleep options, add user accounts, and customize the Dock, to name some of the tasks that you learn about in this chapter.

To use these settings, you must know how to display the System Preferences window.

Display System Preferences

Open System Preferences

1 In the Dock, click **System Preferences** (⚙).

The System Preferences window appears.

Close System Preferences

1 Click **System Preferences**.

2 Click **Quit System Preferences**.

Are there other methods I can use to open and close System Preferences?
If you have hidden the Dock (as described later in the "Hide the Dock" section) or removed the System Preferences icon from the Dock, you can click <img> and then click **System Preferences**. To quit System Preferences, right-click <img> and then click **Quit**. Alternatively, switch to System Preferences and press ⌘ + Q.

Sometimes when I open System Preferences I do not see all the icons. How can I restore the original icons?
When you click an icon in System Preferences, the window changes to show just the options and settings associated with that icon. To return to the main System Preferences window, press ⌘ + L or use either of the following techniques:

- Click ◄ until the main window appears.

- Click **Show All**.

Change the Desktop Background

To give Mac OS X a different look, you can change the default desktop background.

Mac OS X offers a wide variety of desktop background options. For example, Mac OS X comes with several dozen images you can use, from abstract patterns to photos of plants and other natural images. You can also choose a solid color as the desktop background, or you can use one of your own photos.

You can change the desktop background to show either a fixed image or a series of images that change periodically.

Change the Desktop Background

Set a Fixed Background Image

1 Open System Preferences.

Note: See the "Display System Preferences" section, earlier in this chapter.

2 Click **Desktop & Screen Saver**.

*Note: You can also right-click the desktop and then click **Change Desktop Background**.*

The desktop and screen saver preferences appear.

3 Click **Desktop**.

4 Click the image category you want to use.

5 Click the image you want to use as the desktop background.

Your Mac changes the desktop background.

6 If you chose a photo in Step **5**, click **⁝** and then click an option to determine how your Mac displays the photo.

Set a Changing Background Image

1 Click **Change picture** (☐ changes to ☑).

2 Click **⁝** in the pop-up menu and then click how often you want the background image to change.

3 If you want your Mac to choose the periodic image randomly, click **Random order** (☐ changes to ☑).

Your Mac changes the desktop background periodically based on your chosen interval.

Simplify It

When I choose a photo, what is the difference between the various options for displaying the photo?

● **Fill Screen**: Expands the photo by the same amount in all four directions until it fills the entire desktop.

● **Fit to Screen**: Expands the photo in all four directions until the photo is either the same height as the desktop or the same width as the desktop.

● **Stretch to Fill Screen**: Expands the photo in all four directions until it fills the entire desktop.

● **Center**: Displays the photo at its actual size and places the photo in the center of the desktop.

● **Tile**: Repeats your photo multiple times to fill the entire desktop.

Activate the Screen Saver

You can set up Mac OS X to display a *screen saver*, a moving pattern or series of pictures. The screen saver appears after your computer has been idle for a while.

If you leave your monitor on for long stretches while your computer is idle, a faint version of the unmoving image can endure for a while on the screen, a phenomenon known as *persistence*. A screen saver prevents this by displaying a moving image. However, persistence is not a major problem for modern screens, so for the most part you use a screen saver for visual interest.

Activate the Screen Saver

1 Open System Preferences.

Note: *See the "Display System Preferences" section, earlier in this chapter.*

2 Click **Desktop & Screen Saver**.

The desktop and screen saver preferences appear.

3 Click **Screen Saver**.

4 Click the screen saver you want to use.

● A preview of the screen saver appears here.

5 Click and drag the **Start screen saver** slider ($\triangledown$) to set when the screen saver begins.

Note: *The interval you choose is the number of minutes or hours that your Mac must be idle before the screen saver starts.*

● If the screen saver is customizable, click **Options** to configure it.

● If you also want to see the current time when the screen saver is active, click **Show with clock** (☐ changes to ☑).

● If you want to see a different screen saver each time, click **Use random screen saver** (☐ changes to ☑).

Simplify It

What are hot corners and how do I configure them?
A *hot corner* is a corner of your Mac's screen that you have set up to perform some action when you move the mouse (▶) to that corner. To configure hot corners, follow these steps:

① Follow Steps **1** to **4** to select a screen saver.

② Click **Hot Corners**.

System Preferences displays the Active Screen Corners dialog.

③ In each of the four pop-up menus, click ⁞ and then click the action you want to perform when you move ▶ to that corner of the screen.

● For example, in the top right pop-up menu, click ⁞ and then click the action you want to perform when you move ▶ to the top right corner of the screen.

④ Click **OK**.

Set Your Mac's Sleep Options

You can make Mac OS X more energy efficient by configuring parts of your Mac to go into sleep mode automatically when you are not using them.

Sleep mode means that your display or your Mac is in a temporary low-power mode. This saves energy on all Macs, and also saves battery power on a notebook Mac. For example, you can set up Mac OS X to put the display to sleep automatically after a period of inactivity. Similarly, you can configure Mac OS X to put your entire Mac to sleep after you have not used it for a specified amount of time.

Set Your Mac's Sleep Options

Open the Energy Saver Preferences

1. Open System Preferences.

   Note: *See the "Display System Preferences" section, earlier in this chapter.*

2. Click **Energy Saver**.

   The Energy Saver preferences appear.

Set Sleep Options for a Desktop Mac

1. Click and drag ▽ to set the computer sleep timer.

   This specifies the period of inactivity after which your computer goes to sleep.

2. Click and drag ▽ to set the display sleep timer.

   This specifies the period of inactivity after which your display goes to sleep.

Set Sleep Options for a Notebook Mac

① Click **Battery**.

② Click and drag ▽ to set the computer sleep timer for when your Mac is on battery power.

③ Click and drag ▽ to set the display sleep timer for when your Mac is on battery power.

④ Click **Power Adapter**.

⑤ Click and drag ▽ to set the computer sleep timer for when your Mac is plugged in.

⑥ Click and drag ▽ to set the display sleep timer for when your Mac is plugged in.

Simplify It

How do I wake up a sleeping display or computer?
You can wake up the display by moving your mouse. You can wake up the computer by clicking the mouse. You can also wake up the display or your entire Mac by pressing a key such as ⌘, Control, Option, or Shift on your keyboard.

I changed the display sleep timer, and now I never see my screen saver. Why?
You have set the display sleep timer to a time that is less than your screen saver timer. Suppose you have configured the screen saver to appear after 15 minutes. If you set the display sleep timer to a shorter interval, such as 10 minutes, Mac OS X will always put the display to sleep before the screen saver appears.

Change the Display Resolution

You can change the resolution of the Mac OS X display. This enables you to adjust the display for best viewing or for maximum compatibility with whatever application you are using.

Increasing the display resolution is an easy way to create more space on the screen for applications and windows because the objects on the screen appear smaller. Conversely, if you are having trouble reading text on the screen, decreasing the display resolution can help because the screen objects appear larger.

You can change the Mac OS X display resolution using either the System Preferences window or the menu bar.

Change the Display Resolution

Change Resolution via the Display Preferences

1 Open System Preferences.

Note: *See the "Display System Preferences" section, earlier in this chapter.*

2 Click **Displays**.

The Displays preferences appear.

3 Click **Display**.

4 Click the resolution you want to use.

Your Mac adjusts the screen to the new resolution.

● To change the resolution using your Mac's menu bar, as described on the next page, click **Show displays in menu bar** (☐ changes to ☑).

Change Resolution via the Menu Bar

1 Click the **Displays** icon ().

Your Mac opens a menu that shows the most commonly or recently used resolutions.

● The resolution with the check mark (✓) is the current resolution.

2 Click the resolution you want to use.

Your Mac adjusts the screen to the new resolution.

Simplify It

What do the resolution numbers mean?

The numbers are *pixels*, short for picture elements, which are the individual dots that make up what you see on your Mac's screen. The resolution tells you the number of pixels in each row and column. So a resolution of 1024 x 768 means the display is using 1,024-pixel rows and 768-pixel columns.

Why do some resolutions also include the word "stretched"?

Older displays are made with the width-to-height ratio — the *aspect ratio* — set at 4:3. However, new Mac displays have a *widescreen* aspect ratio of 16:10. Resolutions designed for 4:3 displays — such as 1024 x 768 — take up only part of a widescreen display. To make them use the entire display, choose the *stretched* resolution.

Create an App Folder in Launchpad

You can make Launchpad easier to work with by combining two or more icons into a single storage area called an *app folder*.

Mac OS X Lion displays the Launchpad icons in up to 5 rows per screen, with up to 8 icons in each row, so you can have as many as 40 icons in each Launchpad screen. Also, if you have

configured your Mac with a relatively low display resolution, you might see only partial app names in the Launchpad screens.

All of this can make it difficult to locate the app you want. However, by creating app folders, you can organize similar apps and reduce the clutter on the Launchpad screens.

Create an App Folder in Launchpad

1 Click **Launchpad** (🔘).

● Launchpad displays icons for each installed application.

2 Click the dot for the Launchpad screen you want to work with.

3 Use the ➤ to click and drag an icon that you want to include in the folder, and drop it on another icon that you want to include in the same folder.

● Launchpad creates the app folder.

● Launchpad applies a name to the folder based on the type of applications in the folder.

● Launchpad adds the icons to the app folder.

④ To specify a different name, click the name and then type the one you prefer.

⑤ Click the Launchpad screen, outside of the app folder.

● Launchpad displays the app folder.

⑥ To add more icons to the new app folder, use the ↖ to click and drag each icon and drop it on the folder.

Note: *To launch a program from an app folder, click* 🅐*, click the app folder to open it, and then click the program's icon.*

Simplify It

How do I make changes to an app folder once it has been created?
Click 🅐 and then click the app folder to open it. To rename the folder, click the current name, type the new name, and then press `Return`. To rearrange the icons, use the ↖ to drag and drop the apps within the folder. When you are done, click outside the app folder to close it.

How do I remove an icon from an app folder?
Click 🅐 and then click the app folder to open it. Use the ↖ to click and drag the app out of the folder. Launchpad closes the folder, and you can then drop the icon within the Launchpad screen. If you remove all the icons from an app folder, Launchpad deletes the folder.

Add a User Account

You can share your Mac with another person by creating a user account for that person. This enables the person to log on to Mac OS X and use the system.

The new user account is completely separate from your own account. This means that the other person can change settings, create documents, and perform other OS X tasks without interfering with your own settings or data.

For maximum privacy for all users, you should set up each user account with a password.

Add a User Account

1 Open System Preferences.

Note: See the "Display System Preferences" section, earlier in this chapter.

2 Click **Users & Groups**.

In most Mac OS X systems, to modify accounts you must click the **Lock** icon (🔒) and then enter your administrator password (🔒 changes to 🔓).

3 Click **Add** (+).

The New Account dialog appears.

④ Click ⁝ and then click an account type.

⑤ Type the user's name.

⑥ Edit the short user name that Mac OS X creates.

⑦ Type a password for the user.

⑧ Retype the user's password.

⑨ Type a hint that Mac OS X will display if the user forgets the password.

⑩ Click **Create User**.

● Mac OS X adds the user account to the Accounts preferences window.

● To change the picture, click the current image and then either click an existing image or click **Edit Picture**.

Which account type should I use for the new account?
The Standard account type is a good choice because it can make changes only to its own account settings. Avoid the Administrator option because it is a powerful account type that enables the user to make major changes to the system. If the user is a child, consider the Managed with Parental Controls account type, which enables you to place restrictions on the user's actions and on the content the person can view.

Customize the Dock

You can customize various aspects of the Dock by using System Preferences to modify a few Dock options.

For example, you can make the Dock take up less room on the screen by adjusting the size of the Dock. You can also make the Dock a bit easier to use by turning on the Magnification feature, which enlarges Dock icons when you position the mouse pointer over them.

You can also make the Dock easier to access and use by moving it to another part of the screen.

Customize the Dock

1 Open System Preferences.

Note: See the "Display System Preferences" section, earlier in this chapter.

2 Click **Dock**.

*Note: You can also open the Dock preferences by clicking , clicking **Dock**, and then clicking **Dock Preferences**.*

The Dock preferences appear.

3 Click and drag the **Size** ▽ to make the Dock smaller or larger.

● You can also click and drag the Dock divider; drag up to increase the Dock size; drag down to decrease the Dock size.

● System Preferences adjusts the size of the Dock.

Note: If your Dock is already as wide as the screen, dragging the Size slider to the right (toward the Large value) has no effect.

④ Click **Magnification** (☐ changes to ☑).

⑤ Click and drag the **Magnification** slider (▽) to set the magnification level.

● When you position the mouse (▸) over a Dock icon, your Mac magnifies the icon.

⑥ Use the Position on screen options to click where you want the Dock to appear, such as the Left side of the screen (○ changes to ◉).

● Your Mac moves the Dock to the new position.

⑦ In the Minimize windows using pop-up menu, click ⁝ and then click the effect you want your Mac to use when you minimize a window: Genie effect or Scale effect.

Simplify It

Is there an easier method I can use to control some of these preferences?
Yes, you can control these preferences directly from the Dock. For example, to set the Dock size, use the ▸ to click and drag the Dock divider (⬤) left or right.

For the other preferences, right-click the Dock divider. Click **Turn Magnification On** to enable the magnification feature; click **Turn Magnification Off** to disable this feature. To change the Dock position, click **Position on Screen** and then click **Left**, **Bottom**, or **Right**. To set the minimize effect, click **Minimize Using** and then click either **Genie Effect** or **Scale Effect**. Finally, you can also click **Dock Preferences** to open System Preferences's Dock window.

Add an Icon to the Dock

The icons on the Dock are convenient because you can open them with just a single click. You can enhance the convenience of the Dock by adding an icon for an application you use frequently.

The icon remains in the Dock even when the application is closed, so you can always open the application with a single click.

You can add an icon to the Dock even if the program is not currently running.

Add an Icon to the Dock

Add an Icon for a Nonrunning Application

① Click **Finder** (⬜).

② Click **Applications**.

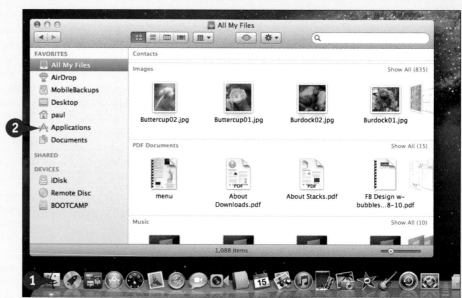

③ Click and drag the application icon, and then drop it inside the Dock.

● Be sure to drop the icon to the left of the Dock divider.

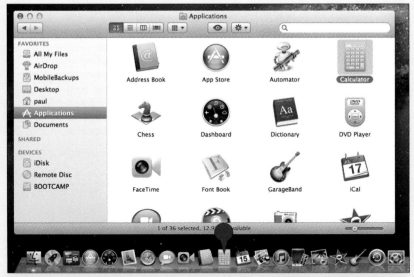

● Mac OS X adds the application's icon to the Dock.

Add an Icon for a Running Application

① Right-click the application icon in the Dock.

② Click **Options**.

③ Click **Keep in Dock**.

The application's icon remains in the Dock even after you close the program.

Simplify It

Is there a way to get my Mac to start the application automatically each time I log in to the computer?
Yes. Your Mac maintains a list of *login items*, which are applications that run automatically after you log in. You can configure your application as a login item, and your Mac opens it automatically each time you log in. Right-click the application's Dock icon, click **Options**, and then click **Open at Login**.

How do I remove an icon from the Dock?
Right-click the application's Dock icon, click **Options**, and then click **Remove from Dock**. If the application is currently running, Mac OS X removes the icon from the Dock when you quit the program. Note that you can remove any application icon except Finder (🗔) and Launchpad (🚀).

Hide the Dock

If you would like more room on the Mac OS X screen to display your applications, you can hide the Dock to free up some screen space.

When you are working in an application, you might find that you need to maximize the amount of vertical space the application window takes up on-screen. This might come up, for example, when you are reading or

editing a long document or viewing a large photo. In such cases, you can size the window to maximum height, but Mac OS X will not let you go past the Dock. You can work around this by hiding the Dock.

When the Dock is hidden, it is still easily accessible whenever you need to use it.

Hide the Dock

Turn On Dock Hiding

1 Click .

2 Click **Dock**.

3 Click **Turn Hiding On**.

● You can also right-click the Dock divider and then click **Turn Hiding On**.

● Mac OS X removes the Dock from the desktop.

Display the Dock Temporarily

① Move the mouse (\) to the bottom of the screen.

● Mac OS X temporarily displays the Dock.

Note: To hide the Dock again, move the mouse (\) away from the bottom of the screen.

Simplify It

Is there a faster way to hide the Dock?
Yes. You can quickly hide the Dock by pressing `Option` + `⌘` + `D`. This keyboard shortcut is a toggle, which means that you can also turn off Dock hiding by pressing `Option` + `⌘` + `D`. When the Dock is hidden, you can display it temporarily by pressing `Control` + `F3` (on some keyboards you must press `Fn` + `Control` + `F3`).

How do I bring the Dock back into view?
When you no longer need the extra screen space for your applications, you can turn off Dock hiding to bring the Dock back into view. Click ●, click **Dock**, and then click **Turn Hiding Off**. Alternatively, display the Dock, right-click the Dock divider, then click **Turn Hiding Off**.

Install a Program Using the App Store

You can enhance and extend Mac OS X by installing new programs from the App Store.

Mac OS X comes with an impressive collection of applications — or *apps* — particularly if your Mac came with the iLife suite preinstalled. However, Mac OS X does not offer a complete collection of apps. For example, Mac OS X lacks apps in categories such as games, personal finance, and social networking.

To fill in these gaps — or to look for apps that go beyond what the default Mac OS X programs can do — you can use the App Store to locate, purchase, and install new programs.

Install a Program Using the App Store

1 In the Dock, click **App Store** (![]).

The App Store window appears.

2 Locate the app you want to install.

3 Click the price button.

Note: *If the app is free, click the Free button instead.*

198

The App Store prompts you to log in with your Apple ID.

④ Type your Apple ID.

⑤ Type your password.

⑥ Click **Sign In**.

The App Store asks you to confirm the purchase.

⑦ Click **Buy**.

● The App Store begins downloading the app.

● When the progress meter disappears, your app is installed. Click Launchpad (⬜) and then click the app to run it.

How do I use an App Store gift card to purchase apps?

If you have an App Store or iTunes gift card, you can redeem the card to give yourself store credit in the amount shown on the card. To redeem the card, first scratch off the sticker on the back to reveal the code. Click ⬜ to open the App Store, click **Redeem** (●), type the code, and then click **Redeem**.

In the App Store window, the Account item (●) shows your current store credit balance.

Quick Links

Welcome Paul
Account $28.36
Redeem
Support

Chapter 11

Performing Mac OS X Maintenance

To keep Mac OS X running smoothly, maintain top performance, and reduce the risk of computer problems, you need to perform some routine maintenance chores. For example, you should empty the Mac OS X Trash folder periodically to save disk space, and you should organize your desktop icons from time to time to reduce clutter. It is also important to keep an eye on your Mac's free disk space to make sure it does not get too low. Finally, it is vital that you configure backups for your Mac to keep your irreplaceable documents safe.

This chapter shows you how to perform these and other maintenance tasks.

Empty the Trash

You can free up disk space on your Mac by periodically emptying the trash.

When you delete a file or folder, Mac OS X does not immediately remove the file from your Mac's hard disk. Instead, Mac OS X moves the file or folder to the Trash. This is useful if you accidentally delete an item because it means

you can open the Trash and restore the item. However, all those deleted files and folders take up disk space, so you need to empty the trash periodically to regain that space.

You should empty the trash at least once a week.

Empty the Trash

1 Click **Finder** (icon).

2 Click **Finder** from the menu.

3 Click **Empty Trash**.

- You can also right-click the **Trash** icon (icon) and then click **Empty Trash**.

  Note: Another way to select the Empty Trash command is to press Shift + ⌘ + Del.

Mac OS X asks you to confirm.

4 Click **Empty Trash**.

Mac OS X empties the trash (icon changes to icon).

Organize Your Desktop

You can make your Mac OS X desktop easier to scan and navigate by organizing the icons.

The Mac OS X desktop automatically displays icons for objects such as your external hard drives, inserted CDs and DVDs, disk images, and attached iPods. The desktop is also a handy place to store files, file aliases, copies of documents, and more.

However, the more you use your desktop as a storage area, the more the desktop can become disarrayed, making it hard to find the icon you want. You can fix this by organizing the icons.

Organize Your Desktop

① Click the desktop.

② Click **View**.

③ Click **Sort By**.

④ Click **Name**.

You can also right-click the desktop, click **Sort By**, and then click **Name**, or press Ctrl + ⌘ + 1.

● If you just want to nudge each icon into the nearest row and column, click **Clean Up** instead.

● Your Mac organizes the icons alphabetically and arranges them in rows and columns from right to left.

Check Hard Disk Free Space

To ensure that your Mac's hard disk does not become full, you should periodically check how much free space it has left.

If you run out of room on your Mac's hard disk, you will not be able to install more applications or create more documents, and your Mac's performance will suffer. To ensure your free space does not become too low —

say, less than about 20 or 25GB — you can check how much free space your hard disk has left.

You should check your Mac's hard disk free space about once a month. If you frequently install programs, create large files, or download media, you should check your free space every couple of weeks.

Check Hard Disk Free Space

Check Free Space Using Finder

① Click **Finder** (image).

② Click your user account folder.

Note: You can also click any folder on your Mac's hard disk.

③ Read the "available" value, which tells you the amount of free space left on the hard disk.

Display Free Space on the Desktop

① Display your Mac's HD (hard drive) icon on the desktop, as described in the first tip on the next page.

② Click the desktop.

③ Click **View**.

④ Click **Show View Options**.

Note: You can also run the Show View Options command by pressing ⌘ + J.

The Desktop dialog appears.

5 Click **Show item info**
(☐ changes to ☑).

● Your Mac displays the amount of free hard disk space under the Macintosh HD icon.

6 Drag the Icon size ▽ until you can read all the icon text.

7 If you still cannot read all the text, click the **Text size** ‡ and then click a smaller size.

8 Click **Close** (●).

Simplify It

My Mac's hard disk icon does not appear on the desktop. How do I display it?
If you do not see the Macintosh HD icon on your desktop, click the desktop, click **Finder** in the menu bar, and then click **Preferences**. Click the **General** tab, click **Hard disks** (☐ changes to ☑), and then click **Close** (●).

Show these items on the desktop:
☑ Hard disks
☑ External disks
☑ CDs, DVDs, and iPods
☐ Connected servers

What should I do if my Mac's hard disk space is getting low?
First, empty the trash, as described earlier in this chapter. Next, uninstall any applications that you no longer use, as described in the next section. If you have documents that you no longer need — particularly large media files — either move them to an external hard disk or USB flash drive, or send them to the Trash and then empty the trash.

Uninstall Unused Applications

If you have an application that you no longer use, you can free up some disk space and reduce clutter in the Applications folder by uninstalling that application.

When you install an application, the program stores its files on your Mac's hard disk, and although most programs are quite small, many require hundreds of megabytes of disk space. Uninstalling applications you do not need frees up the disk space they use and removes their icons or folders from the Applications folder.

In most cases you must be logged on to Mac OS X with an administrator account to uninstall applications.

Uninstall Unused Applications

1 Click **Finder** (⌘).

2 Click **Applications**.

3 Click and drag the application or its folder and drop it on the **Trash** icon (🗑).

If your Mac prompts you for an administrator password, type the password, and then click **OK**.

● Your Mac uninstalls the application.

Is there another way to uninstall an application?

A few Mac applications come with a separate program for uninstalling the application:

1 Follow Steps **1** to **3**.

2 If the application has its own folder, examine the contents for an icon with "Uninstaller" in the name.

3 Double-click that icon and then follow the instructions on-screen.

Set a Software Update Schedule

You can ensure that your Mac and the applications that come with Mac OS X are up to date with the latest features and fixes by setting a schedule for updating the software.

Apple makes Mac OS X updates available from time to time. These updates fix problems, add new features, and resolve security issues. You can reduce computer problems and maximize online safety by setting up Mac OS X to download and install these updates automatically.

By default, Mac OS X checks for updates weekly. You can configure Software Update to check for updates daily or only once a month.

Set a Software Update Schedule

1 Click .

2 Click **System Preferences**.

Note: You can also click ***System Preferences*** (📷) in the Dock.

The System Preferences window appears.

3 Click **Software Update**.

The Software Update preferences appear.

④ Click **Scheduled Check**.

⑤ Click **Check for updates** (☐ changes to ☑).

⑥ In the Check for updates pop-up menu, click ⁝ and then click the schedule you want: **Daily**, **Weekly**, or **Monthly**.

⑦ Click **Download updates automatically** (☐ changes to ☑).

Your Mac checks for updates on your selected schedule, and downloads updates automatically.

How does Software Update work?
When the time comes for an update check, Software Update first examines what Apple applications and system software you have installed on your Mac. Then, for each program, Software Update queries an Internet database on Apple's site to see if the program has an update available. If it does, Software Update adds the program to the update list. If the update is considered important, Software Update immediately downloads the update. The Software Update icon then bounces in the Dock to let you know that updates are available.

Configure Time Machine Backups

One of the most crucial Mac OS X maintenance chores is to configure your system to make regular backups of your files. Macs are reliable machines, but they do crash and all hard disks eventually die, so at some point your data will be at risk. To avoid losing that data forever, you need to configure the Mac OS X Time Machine feature to perform regular backups.

To use Time Machine, your Mac requires a second hard disk. This can be a second internal disk on a Mac Pro, but on most Macs the easiest course is to connect an external hard disk, which is what this task assumes.

Configure Time Machine Backups

① Connect an external USB or FireWire hard disk to your Mac.

● When your Mac recognizes the external hard disk, it adds an icon for the disk to the desktop.

Note: *If you do not see the icon, click* **Finder**, *click* **Preferences**, *and then click* **External Disks** *(□ changes to ☑).*

② Click .

③ Click **System Preferences**.

Note: *You can also click* **System Preferences** *(☒) in the Dock.*

Note: *If Mac OS X asks if you want to use the hard disk as your backup disk, click* **Use as Backup Disk** *and then skip the rest of these steps.*

④ Click **Time Machine**.

The Time Machine preferences appear.

5 Click **Select Disk**.

Time Machine displays a list of available disks.

6 Click the external hard disk.

7 Click **Use Backup Disk**.

Time Machine enables backups and prepares to run the first backup automatically in 2 minutes.

8 Click **Close** (●).

How do Time Machine backups work?
Time Machine backups use the following schedule:

- The initial backup occurs 2 minutes after you configure Time Machine. This backup includes your entire Mac.
- Time Machine runs an hourly backup that includes just those files and folders that you have changed or created since the most recent hourly backup.
- Time Machine runs a daily backup that includes only those files and folders that you have changed or created since the most recent daily backup.
- Time Machine runs a weekly backup that includes only those files and folders that you have changed or created since the most recent weekly backup.

Restore Files Using Time Machine

If you have configured Mac OS X to make regular Time Machine backups, you can use those backups to restore a lost file.

If you accidentally delete a file, you can quickly restore it by opening the Trash folder. However, that does not help you if you have emptied the Trash folder, if you overwrite a file with another

file with the same name, or if you improperly edit a file.

Because Time Machine makes hourly, daily, and weekly backups, it stores older copies and older versions of your data. You can use these backups to restore any file that you accidentally delete, overwrite, or improperly edit.

Restore Files Using Time Machine

1 Click **Finder** (icon).

2 Open the folder you want to restore, or the folder that contains the file you want to restore.

3 Click **Time Machine** (icon).

The Time Machine interface appears.

● Each window represents a backed-up version of the folder.

● This area tells you when the displayed version of the folder was backed up.

● You can use this timeline to navigate the backed-up versions.

4 Navigate to the date that contains the backed-up version of the folder or file.

Note: *See the tip below to learn how to navigate the Time Machine backups.*

5 If you are restoring a file, click the file.

6 Click **Restore**.

If another version of the folder or file already exists, Time Machine asks if you want to keep it or replace it.

7 Click **Replace**.

Time Machine restores the folder or file.

How do I navigate the backups in the Time Machine interface?
Here are the most useful techniques:

● Click the top arrow to jump to the earliest version; click the bottom arrow to return to the most recent version.

● Press and hold the ⌘ key and click the arrows to navigate through the backups one version at a time.

● Use the timeline to click a specific version.

● Click the version windows.

Chapter 12

Troubleshooting Mac OS X Problems

Mac OS X Lion is a solid operating system, and it should give you many years of dependable performance. However, *all* computers eventually run into problems, and your Mac will likely be no exception. To help you get through these inevitable rough patches, this chapter offers a few tried-and-true troubleshooting techniques.

For example, you begin by learning easy troubleshooting techniques such as how to restart your Mac and how to unlock System Preferences. You also learn how to force a crashed application to quit, how to repair a corrupt preferences file, and how to reset your Mac's password. This chapter also shows you how to repair disk permissions and how to repair a disk.

Restart Your Mac

If a hardware device is having a problem with some system files, it often helps to restart your Mac. By rebooting the computer, you reload the entire system, which is often enough to solve many computer problems.

For a problem device that does not have its own power switch, restarting your Mac might not resolve the problem because the device remains powered up the whole time. You can *power cycle* — shut down and then restart — such devices as a group by power cycling your Mac.

Restart Your Mac

Restart Your Mac

1 Click the **Apple** icon (🍎).

2 Click **Restart**.

Your Mac asks you to confirm.

3 Click **Restart**.

Note: *To bypass the confirmation dialog, press and hold* Option *when you click the* **Restart** *command.*

Power Cycle Your Mac

1️⃣ Click .

2️⃣ Click **Shut Down**.

Your Mac asks you to confirm.

Note: *To bypass the confirmation dialog, hold down* Option *when you click **Shut Down**.*

3️⃣ Click **Shut Down**.

4️⃣ Wait for 30 seconds to give all devices time to spin down.

5️⃣ Turn your Mac back on.

What other basic troubleshooting techniques can I use?

- Make sure that each device is turned on, that cable connections are secure, and that insertable devices (such as USB devices) are properly inserted.

- If a device is battery powered, replace the batteries.

- If a device has an on/off switch, power cycle the device by turning it off, waiting a few seconds for it to stop spinning, and then turning it back on again.

- Close all running programs.

- Log out of your Mac — click ; click **Log Out *User***, where *User* is your Mac user name; and then click **Log Out** — and then log back in again.

Unlock System Preferences

When you open System Preferences and click an icon, you may find that some or all of the controls in the resulting preferences window are disabled. To enable those controls, you need to unlock the preferences.

Remember that having locked system preferences is not a glitch. Instead, it is a security feature designed to prevent unauthorized users from making changes to sensitive system settings.

After you unlock most system preferences, Mac OS X automatically locks them again when you exit the System Preferences application.

Unlock System Preferences

1 Click **System Preferences** (◉) in the Dock.

The System Preferences window appears.

2 Click the icon of the system preferences you want to work with (such as Users & Groups, as shown here).

The preferences appear.

3 Click the **System Preferences Locked** icon (🔒).

System Preferences prompts you for an administrator's user name and password.

④ Use the Name text box to type the name of an administrator account on your Mac.

⑤ Use the Password text box to type the administrator account's password.

⑥ Click **Unlock**.

● 🔒 changes to 🔓.

● Your Mac enables the preferences.

Some preferences are already unlocked. Should I lock them?
Locking system preferences prevents unauthorized changes to those preferences. If you are the only person who uses your Mac, you can leave those system preferences unlocked for convenience. However, if other people have access to your Mac, you should lock important system preferences by clicking 🔓 (which changes to 🔒).

Is there a way to lock my entire Mac?
You can configure your Mac to require a password when it wakes up from sleep mode or from the screen saver. Click **System Preferences** (⚙) in the Dock, click **Security & Privacy**, click 🔒, and then type a password. Click **General**, click **Require password** (☐ changes to ☑), click ⬍, and then click **immediately**.

Force a Stuck Application to Close

When you are working with an application, you may find that it becomes unresponsive and you cannot interact with the application or even quit the application normally. In that case, you can use a Mac OS X feature called Force Quit to force a stuck or unresponsive application to close, which enables you to restart the application or restart your Mac.

Unfortunately, when you force an application to quit, you lose any unsaved changes in your open documents. Therefore, make sure the application really is stuck before forcing it to quit. See the second tip on the following page for more information.

Force a Stuck Application to Close

① Click .

② Click **Force Quit**.

The Force Quit Applications window appears.

③ Click the application you want to shut down.

④ Click **Force Quit**.

Your Mac asks you to confirm that you want to force the application to quit.

⑤ Click **Force Quit**.

Your Mac shuts down the application.

⑥ Click **Close** (●) to close the Force Quit Applications window.

Are there easier ways to run the Force Quit command?
Yes. From the keyboard, you can run the Force Quit command by pressing Option + ⌘ + Esc. If the application has a Dock icon, press and hold Control + Option and then click the application's Dock icon. In the menu that appears, click **Force Quit**.

If an application is not responding, does that always mean the application is stuck?
Not necessarily. For example, some application operations — such as recalculating a large spreadsheet or rendering a 3-D image — can take a few minutes, and during that time the application can appear stuck. Similarly, your Mac may be low on memory, which can also cause an application to seem stuck. In this case, try shutting down some other applications to free up some memory.

Repair a Corrupt Preferences File

You can use Mac OS X to reset an application's preferences file, which may help you solve problems you may be having with the application.

One of the most common causes of application instability is a preferences file that has somehow become corrupted. Although there is no easy way to fix a corrupt preferences file directly, you can so do indirectly by deleting the preferences file. The next time you start the application, the application detects that its preferences file is missing, so it automatically rebuilds a new — and uncorrupted — file. The downside to this method is that you may have to reconfigure the application's preferences.

Repair a Corrupt Preferences File

1 If the problem application is still running, shut it down.

> **Note:** If you have trouble closing the application, see the section "Force a Stuck Application to Close."

2 Click **Finder** (🖼).

3 Click your user account folder.

4 Click **Go**.

5 Click **Go to Folder**.

The Go to Folder dialog appears.

6 Type **~/Library/Preferences**.

7 Click **Go**.

The Preferences folder appears.

8 Click and drag the problem application's preferences file and drop it on the Trash.

Note: *See the second tip below to learn how to locate the correct preferences file.*

Your Mac deletes the preferences file.

9 Run the application and set some preferences.

● The application creates a new preferences file.

Simplify It

What is a preferences file?
It is a document that stores a user's options, settings, and other data related to a particular application. To specify preferences, click the application's name in the menu bar and then click **Preferences**. The application displays a dialog that you use to customize the preferences. The application saves the new settings in the preferences file.

How can I tell which preferences file belongs to the problem application?
Most preferences files use the .plist filename extension. In most cases, the filename uses the following general format: com.*company.application*.plist. Here, *company* is the name of the software company that makes the application, and *application* is the name of the program. Here are some examples: com.apple.iTunes.plist; com.microsoft. Word.plist; com.palm.HotSync.plist.

Access the Mac OS X Recovery Tools

You can recover from some Mac problems by accessing the recovery tools that are available on systems running Mac OS X Lion.

All Macs that have Mac OS X Lion installed have a hidden area of the hard drive called Recovery HD, which contains a program called Mac OS X Utilities. This program offers various tools that you can use to troubleshoot and recover from problems. For example, if you suspect that your Mac's main hard drive is causing a problem, you can access Recovery HD and use a tool called Disk Utility to repair the drive. Similarly, you can also use Recovery HD to restore your Mac from a Time Machine backup, and to reinstall Mac OS X Lion.

Access the Mac OS X Recovery Tools

Start Mac OS X Utilities

1 Restart your Mac.

2 Press and hold **Option** while your Mac is restarting.

A list of disk drives appears.

3 Double-click **Recovery HD**.

The Mac OS X Utilities application appears.

Restart Your Mac

1 Click .

2 Click **Restart**.

● If you prefer to turn off your Mac instead, click **Shut Down**.

Simplify It

If I cannot start my Mac, is there any way to access troubleshooting information on the web?

Yes. You can start your Mac using Recovery HD and then use the Mac OS X Utilities to access the web.

First, you must connect to your Wi-Fi network so that you can access its Internet connection. Click the **Wi-Fi Status** icon (), click your Wi-Fi network, and then type your Wi-Fi password, if prompted.

In the Mac OS X Utilities window, click **Get Help Online** and then click **Continue**. Mac OS X Utilities loads Safari and displays some troubleshooting steps. However, you can also use Safari to surf to any site that has the information you seek.

Repair Disk Permissions

Your Mac's files can become corrupted for a variety of reasons. For example, a hard disk glitch could render a file impossible to read; similarly, if Mac OS X or an application crashes, one or more files could develop problems.

If the permissions on one or more of your Mac's system files become corrupted, your Mac may freeze, run slowly, or become unstable. You can often solve these Mac OS X problems by repairing the permissions associated with each file and folder on your Mac's hard disk.

Repair Disk Permissions

1 Click **Finder** ().

2 Click **Applications**.

3 Open the Utilities folder.

   Note: *You can also open the Utilities folder by pressing* Shift + ⌘ + U.

The Utilities folder opens.

4 Double-click **Disk Utility**.

The Disk Utility window appears.

⑤ Click your Mac's hard disk.

⑥ Click **First Aid**.

⑦ Click **Repair Disk Permissions**.

Your Mac repairs the disk permissions.

⑧ When the repair is complete, press ⌘ + Q to quit Disk Utility.

Simplify It

What are disk permissions?
Permissions are settings that determine what users can do with each file. For example, if read-only permissions apply to a file, it means that users can only read the contents of the file and cannot make any changes to the file. If the permissions for your Mac's system files change or get corrupted, it can cause problems, including application lock-ups and unstable system behavior.

How do I repair permissions if I cannot start my Mac?
Corrupt disk permissions might prevent your Mac from booting. In this case, follow Steps **1** to **3** in the "Access the Mac OS X Recovery Tools" section, click **Disk Utility**, click **Continue**, and then follow Steps **5** to **7** in this section.

Repair a Disk

You can use your Mac OS X install DVD to check for errors on your Mac's hard disk and repair those errors.

If your Mac will not start, or if an application freezes, an error on the main hard disk is possibly causing the problem. To see if this is the case, you can try repairing the hard disk using Disk Utility, which you can find in the Utilities folder within your Applications folder.

To repair your Mac's main hard drive, you need to have the original installation DVD that came with your Mac or that you used to install Mac OS X.

Repair a Disk

① Restart your Mac.

② Press and hold **Option** while your Mac is restarting.

A list of disk drives appears.

③ Double-click **Recovery HD**.

The Mac OS X Utilities application appears.

④ Click **Disk Utility**.

⑤ Click **Continue**.

The Disk Utility window appears.

6 Click your Mac's hard disk.

7 Click **First Aid**.

8 Click **Repair Disk**.

Disk Utility verifies the hard disk and attempts to repair any errors it finds.

● Information on the disk checks appears here.

● The result of the checks appears here.

9 Click .

10 Click **Restart**.

Your Mac restarts.

Simplify It

How do I repair errors on a secondary hard disk?
For hard disks other than your Mac's startup disk, you can perform the repair without rebooting. Click **Finder** ( ), click **Applications**, click **Utilities**, and then double-click **Disk Utility**. Click the disk you want to repair, click **First Aid**, and then click **Repair Disk**.

What do I do if Disk Utility finds a problem?
In the best-case scenario, Disk Utility reports either "No repairs were necessary" or "The volume Macintosh HD appears to be OK." Otherwise, Disk Utility attempts to fix any errors it finds. If Disk Utility cannot fix the errors, you must turn to a third-party disk repair application. Two useful tools are DiskWarrior (www.alsoft.com) and TechTool Pro (www.micromat.com).

Index

Index

Index

Index

Index

Index

Index

Read Less–Learn More®

Visual

There's a Visual book
for every learning level...

Simplified®

The place to start if you're new to computers. Full color.

- Computers
- Creating Web Pages
- Digital Photography
- Excel
- Internet
- Laptops
- Mac OS
- Office
- PCs
- Windows
- Word

Teach Yourself VISUALLY™

Get beginning to intermediate-level training in a variety of topics. Full color.

- Access
- Algebra
- Astronomy
- Bass Guitar
- Beadwork
- Bridge
- Car Care and Maintenance
- Chess
- Circular Knitting
- Collage & Altered Art
- Computers
- Crafting with Kids
- Crocheting
- Digital Photography
- Digital Video
- Dog Training
- Drawing
- Dreamweaver
- Excel
- Flash
- Golf
- Guitar
- Hand Dyeing
- Handspinning
- HTML
- iLife
- iPad
- iPhone
- iPhoto
- Jewelry Making & Beading
- Knitting
- Lightroom
- Macs
- Mac OS
- Office
- Outlook
- Photoshop
- Photoshop Elements
- Piano
- Poker
- PowerPoint
- Quilting
- Scrapbooking
- Sewing
- Web Design
- Windows
- Wireless Networking
- Word
- WordPress

Top 100 Simplified® Tips & Tricks

Tips and techniques to take your skills beyond the basics. Full color.

- Digital Photography
- eBay
- Excel
- Google
- Office
- Photoshop
- Photoshop Elements
- PowerPoint
- Windows